A STUDENT
OF THE END TIMES
PROPHECIES
INTERPRETATION OF BIBLE PROPHECIES

A STUDENT
OF THE END TIMES
PROPHECIES
INTERPRETATION OF BIBLE PROPHECIES

DR. EBENEZER KYERE NKANSAH

XULON PRESS ELITE

Xulon Press Elite
2301 Lucien Way #415
Maitland, FL 32751
407.339.4217
www.xulonpress.com

Editor - Alastair Tucker
Contact: +233-260-719-303
alastair.l.tucker@gmail,com
LinkedIn: gh.linkedin.com/pub/alastair.tucker/5/5bb/575

Printed in the United States of America.

ISBN-13: 978-1-5456-7331-7

Dedication

I am dedicating this book to my lovely wife Sarah Adwoa Agyeiwaa. You have been so helpful during the time of writing this book. You gave me more of your time to make this creation successful.

Acknowledgment

All Glory to my Lord Jesus
for giving the revelation to this wonderful work.

Table of Contents

About this Book

T his is a revised model of A Student of Prophecy; now as A Student of the End Times Prophecies.
I am still asking questions about why over 90% messages in churches, on televisions, audios and social media are silent about the preaching and teaching of the End Times Prophecies? The answers to these questions are my challenge. This will, however, help shape the minds of fellow ministers, leaders and Christians, who may need such information to preach and to teach as well.

This is a student's handbook and teaches in-depth knowledge of the end times prophetic interpretation. It talks about the things Jesus said would happen before His Second Coming and the End Time prophecies of the Old Testament which remain to be fulfilled. How are they going to happen, where and when are they going to happen and who are going to be used to make them happen? By the time you finished reading this book you will be able to compare and find answers for yourself. (Matthew 24:1-51)

Contact Information
Website: www.hognetwork.org
Email: Kyerenkansah@yahoo.com
        Kyerenkansah2@gmail.com
        Hopeofgloryi@yahoo.org
Tel: +1-347-559-9329

About the Author

D r. Ebenezer Kyere Nkansah holds a doctorate Degree in Christian Education of Theology and Doctor of Divinity from International Miracle Institute, Pensacola Florida.

He is the founder of Hope of Glory Network Ministries, Hope of Glory Baptist Church, and the CEO of the Hope of Glory Network Radio, in Maryland, USA. A Lecturer/Administrator at Pentecostal International Bible Seminary; Writer/ Motivational /Conferences and Workshops Speaker.
"In most of our churches today, there is silence on end time prophecy. This book seeks to redress that omission. As a researcher of end times prophecies and student of Apologetics, Dr. Kyere Nkansah is well qualified to correct misunderstandings based on all too common false prophetic teachings."

1

The Times of the Gentiles

T he Times of the Gentiles simply means the period in Israel's history as a nation, started in Egypt, to the Second Coming of Jesus Christ, when Israel will be oppressed by "Gentiles" or Non-Jewish nationals. It started with the Egyptians bondage by the Pharaohs, and not with the overthrow of Jerusalem by Nebuchadnezzar. That includes stages and period of times in which the world we live in today used to have one world leadership, as its president. There will be another world president before the return and coming of Jesus Christ.

> "And they will fall by the edge of the sword and be led away captive into all nations. And Jerusalem will be trampled on by the Gentiles until The Times of The Gentiles are fulfilled". (Luke 21:24).

Nebuchadnezzar's Dream

Daniel 2

The Times

of the

Gentiles

606 BC
Babylonian
Empire

538 BC
Medo-Persian
Empire

333 BC
Grecian
Empire

63 BC
Rome
(not named)

Approximately where we are today

Christ

The Genesis of the Gentiles Dominion

> "And he said unto Abram, know of a surety that thy
> seed shall be a stranger in a land that is not theirs,
> and shall serve them; and they shall afflict them
> four hundred years; And also, that nation, whom
> they shall serve, will I judge and afterward shall
> they come out with great substance. And thou shalt
> go to thy fathers in peace; thou shalt be buried in a
> good old age. But in the fourth generation they shall
> come hither again: for the iniquity of the Amorites
> is not yet full. And it came to pass, that, when the
> sun went down, and it was dark, behold a smoking
> furnace, and a burning lamp that passed between
> those pieces. In the same day the Lord made a cove-
> nant with Abram, saying, unto thy seed have I given
> this land, from the river of Egypt unto the great
> river, the river Euphrates." (Genesis 15:13-18 KJV)

God gave the above prophetic message to Abraham and when the
time came for the prophecy to be fulfilled, Joseph, the fourth generation from Abraham, and a grandson was sold by his own brother
to Egyptian slave master Potiphar.

17th Prophecy in Genesis 15:13-16.

This Predicts that Abraham's seed would be sojourners for 400
years more: that Egypt would be punished for enslaving Israel;
that Israel would become very rich: that Abraham would live
long: and that his seed would come out of Egypt in the 4th generation to defeat the Amorites. This prophecy was fulfilled in
the Exodus and settlement of Canaan under Moses and Joshua.
(Exodus 7:1-14:28; Numbers 21:21-25; Joshua 12).

The actual sojourn of Abraham's seed in Egypt was 215 years.
There were other countries which made up the land of sojourn

(Genesis 12:1-20; 13:1-18; 15:13-14; 20:1-18; 21:22-34; 23:4; 26:23-35; 2810; 29:1; 31:13-55; 35:6; 37:1; 46:1-7; 47:27; 50:22-26; Exodus 1-12; Hebrews 11:8-10). The 400 years of Genesis 15:13 and Acts 7:6 date back to the time when Isaac was weaned and confirmed as the seed, and Ishmael was cast out. (Genesis 21:12; Galatians 4:30). At that time Isaac was 5 years old.

Other scriptures speak of the period as 430 years. (Exodus 12:40; Galatians 3:14-17), and that reckoning dates back farther, to take in the 5 years of Isaac's life and 25 years before his birth – when Abraham went into Canaan to sojourn.

The following outline shows how the 430 years are accounted for. Subtracting the 30 years (25 for Abraham's sojourn before Isaac and 5 years for Isaac's years before he was confirmed as the seed) explains the 400 years.

How the 430 Years Are Reckoned:	Years
1. From 75 years of Abraham to birth of Isaac (Genesis 12:4; 21:5)	25
2. From Isaac's birth to that of Jacob (Genesis 25:26)	60
3. From Jacob's birth to his death (Genesis 47:28)	147
4. From Jacob's death to that of Joseph (Genesis 37:2; 41:46; 47:28; 50:22)	54
5. From Joseph's death to the exodus from Egypt (Genesis12:40; Galatians 3:14-17	144
Total	430

(The Dake Annotated Bible, KJV, Red Letter Edition. Page 13 Colum 1 o)

Who are the Gentiles?

The term Gentile referred to a non-Jewish people. Goy is from the Latin "gentilis", by the French "gentil", feminine: "gentile", meaning of or belonging to a clan or tribe that is commonly means non-Jewish. Other groups that claim Israelite heritage sometimes use the term to describe outsiders.

Paul gave admonition to remind Christians of our origin and background as Gentiles:

> "Therefore, remember that at one-time you Gentiles in the flesh, called "the uncircumcision" by what is called the circumcision, which is made in by hands–remember that you were at that time separated from Christ, alienated from the commonwealth of Israel and strangers to the covenants of promise, having no hope and without God in the world." (Ephesians 2:11-12)

It is a fact that, the Jews were oppressed under Egypt: "but the more they were oppressed the more they multiplied and spread, so it happened that the Egyptians came to dread the Israelites."

"And now the cry of the Israelites has reached me, and I have seen the way Egyptians are oppressing them." (Exodus 1:12; 3:9) Assyria was next to oppressed Israel more than 1,500 years off and on before Nebuchadnezzar's invasion in 606 BC.

What would Oppression by the Times of The Gentiles Be?

The books of Revelation and Daniel give the clear picture of what would be the oppression of the Gentiles. We shall investigate them in later chapters.

Revelation 17:8-17 proves that these have been and will be eight (8) great world empires to oppress Israel particularly in the present generation, before the second coming of Jesus Christ.

"The beast that you saw was, and is not, and about to rise from the
bottomless pit and go destruction. And the dwellers on earth whose
names have not been written in the book of life from the foundation of the world will marvel to see the beast, because it was and
is not and is to come. This calls for a mind with wisdom: the seven
heads are seven mountains on which the woman is seated. They
are also seven kings, five of whom have fallen, one is, the other
has not yet come, and when he does come, he must remain only a
little while. As for the beast that was and is not, it is an eight, but
it belongs to the seven, and goes to destruction. And the ten horns
that you saw are ten kings who have not yet received royal power,
but they are to receive authority as kings for one hour, together with
the beast. These are of one mind and they hand over their power
and authority to the beast. They will make war on the Lamb, and
the Lamb will conquer them, for he is Lord of lords and King of
kings, and those with him are called and chosen and faithful. And
the angel said to me, the waters that you saw, where the prostitute
is seated are people and multitudes and nations and languages. And
the ten horns that you saw, they and the beast, these will hate the
prostitute. They will make her desolate and naked and devour her
flesh and burn her up with fire. For God has put it into their hearts
to carry out his purpose by being of one mind and handing over
their royal power to the beast until the words of God are fulfilled."
(Revelation 17:8-17)

The beast on which the woman sat was a seat of idolatry and persecution and is not at John's time; not in the ancient form, which
was pagan: yet it is; it is truly the seat of idolatry and tyranny,
though of another sort and form. It would deceive into stupid and
blind submission all the inhabitants of the earth within its influence,
except the remnant of the elect. This beast was seven heads, seven
mountains, the seven hills on which Rome stands, and seven kings,
seven sorts of government. Five had gone by when this prophecy
was written; one was then in being; the other was yet to come. The
beast directed by the papacy, makes an eighth governor, and sets up
idolatry again. It had ten horns, which are said to ten kings who had
yet no kingdoms; they should not rise until the Roman Empire was

broken; but should for a time be very zealous in her interest. Christ must reign until all enemies be put under his feet. The reason of the victory is, that he is the King of kings, and Lords of lords. He has supreme dominion and power over all things; all the powers of earth and hell are subject to his control. His followers are called to this warfare, are fitted for it, and will be faithful in it.

(Matthew Henry's concise Commentary on the whole Bible. Page 1285, Revelation 17:7-14, Colum 1.)

The time of the Gentiles will end at the return of the Messiah in Glory when He will deliver Israel from the Gentiles and exalt them as head of all nations in the millennium forever. (Luke 21:24; Romans 11:25; Revelation 19:11-20)

God rules this universe with time on a systematic timetable schedule although, this world, is controlled and is still being ruled by the Gentiles. The fullness of all inequity is coming to an end soon when the leaders of this world will no longer be able to take decisions. The Times of the Gentiles are ending so soon and repentance to receive Jesus Christ as Lord and Savior is the only remedy to escape the full wrath and judgment of God. Paul addressed the Jews in Rome this way:

> "For I would not, brethren, that ye should be ignorant of this mystery, lest ye should be wise in your own conceits; that blindness in part is happened to Israel, until the fullness of the Gentiles be come in." (Romans 11:25 KJV).

The Abomination of Desolation

The phrase *"abomination of desolation"* referred to in Matthew 25:15 is a direct reference to Daniel's prophecy more than 2500 years ago.

"So when you see the abomination of desolation spoken of by the prophet Daniel, standing in the holy place (let the reader understand)," (Matthew 24:15)

"And he shall make a strong covenant with many for one week, and for half of the week he shall put an end to sacrifice and offering. And on the wing of abominations shall come one who makes desolate, until the decreed end is poured out on the desolator." (Daniel 9:27)

Antiochus Epiphanies IV

In 167 BC, a Greek ruler emerged by the name of Antiochus Epiphanies IV. He set up an altar to Zeus over the altar of the burnt offering in the Jewish Temple in Jerusalem. He also sacrifices a pig (the abomination) on the altar in the Temple in Jerusalem. This is even called "abomination of desolation. After some 200 years later, Jesus illustrated a prophetical reference in his teachings to his disciples regarding the end time prior to his second coming, (Matthew 24:15; Daniel 9:27). In this context, Jesus said that, a repetition of something like that of the abomination of desolation would be seen in the Jewish Temple in Jerusalem.

This is how the history of Maccabees recorded it:

Abolition of Judaism.

"Not long after this the king sent an Athenian senator to force the Jews to abandon the laws of their ancestors and live no longer by the laws of God, also to profane the temple in Jerusalem and dedicate it to Olympian Zeus, and the one on Mount Gerizim to Zeus the Host to Strangers, as the local inhabitants were wont to be. This was a harsh and utterly intolerable evil. The Gentiles filled the temple with debauchery and revelry; they amused themselves with prostitutes and had intercourse with women even in the sacred courts. They also brought forbidden things into the temple, so that the altar was covered with abominable offerings prohibited by the laws.

No one could keep the Sabbath or celebrate the traditional feasts, nor even admit being a Jew. Moreover, at the monthly celebration of the king's birthday the Jews, from bitter necessity, had to partake of the sacrifices, and when the festival of Dionysus was celebrated, they were compelled to march in his procession, wearing wreaths of ivy.

Following upon a vote of the citizens of Ptolemais, a decree was issued ordering the neighboring Greek cities to adopt the same measures, obliging the Jews to partake of the sacrifices and putting to death those who would not consent to adopt the customs of the Greeks. It was obvious, therefore, that disaster had come upon them. Thus, two women who were arrested for having circumcised their children were publicly paraded about the city with their babies hanging at their breasts and then thrown down from the top of the city wall. Others, who had assembled in nearby caves to observe the seventh day in secret, were betrayed to Philip and all burned to death. In their respect for the holiness of that day, they refrained from defending themselves." (2 Maccabees 6:1-11 New American Bible (Revised Edition) (NABRE) page 672)

Many scholars believe Jesus was talking about the future Antichrist who will do something similar to what Antiochus Epiphanies did. This is confirmed by the fact that, some of what Daniel prophesied in Daniel 9:27 did not occur in 167 BC with Antiochus Epiphanies.

Antiochus did not confirm a covenant with Israel for seven years (one week). It is the future Antiochus (Antichrist) who will establish a covenant with Israel for seven years and then break it in three and half years and doing something like the abomination of desolation in the Jewish third Temple in Jerusalem. It is understood by

John that no matter who and where that person may come from; will be the future Antichrist.

> "And by the signs that it is allowed to work in the presence of the beast it deceives those who dwell on earth, telling them to make an image for the beast that was wounded by the sword and yet lived." (Revelation 13:14)

> "But stay awake at all times, praying that you may have strength to escape all these things that are going to take place, and to stand before the Son of Man." (Luke 21:36)

2

The Temple of Israel in Jerusalem

P resident Trump of The United States of America on Wednesday, December 6, 2017, formally recognized Jerusalem as the capital of Israel, reversing nearly seven decades of American foreign policy and setting in motion a plan to move the United States Embassy from Tel Aviv to the fiercely contested Holy City.

"Today we finally acknowledge the obvious: that Jerusalem is Israel's capital," Mr. Trump said from the Diplomatic Reception Room of the White House. "This is nothing than a recognition of reality. It is also the right thing to do. It's something that has to be done."

The president cast his decision as a break with decades of failed policy on Jerusalem, which the United States, along with virtually every other nation in the world, has declined to recognize as the capital since Israel's founding in 1948. That policy, he said, brought us "no closer to a lasting peace agreement between Israel and the Palestinians."

"It would be folly to assume that repeating the exact same formula would now produce a different or better result," Mr. Trump declared.

Recognizing Jerusalem, he added, was "a long overdue step to advance the peace process."

Mr. Trump's remarks were the most closely scrutinized of his presidency on the Middle East, where he has vowed to broker the "ultimate deal" between Israelis and Palestinians but has yet to find a breakthrough to end the conflict. He said he remained committed to brokering an agreement "that is a great deal for the Israelis and a great deal for the Palestinians."

(https://www.nytimes.com/2017/12/06/world/middleeast/ trump-jerusalem-israel-capital.html)

It is obvious that Jerusalem should be recognized as the capital of Israel to pave way for the construction of the new Jewish Temple. There had been history from the building of the Tabernacle of the tent of Moses to the building of the Solomon's Temple in Jerusalem. Until 1948 from AD 70, the Jews had not lived in their own land that God gave to their ancestors as inheritance in the land of Palestine.

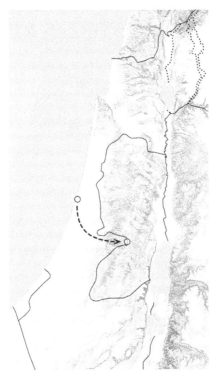

Historic Palestine Israel Map

1. Solomon's Temple "The First Temple in Jerusalem"

According to the Hebrew Bible, Solomon's Temple, also known as the First Temple, was the Holy Temple in ancient Jerusalem before its destruction by Nebuchadnezzar II after the Siege of Jerusalem of 587 BC and its subsequent replacement with the Second Temple in the 6th century BC.

The Hebrew Bible states that the temple was constructed under Solomon, king of the United Kingdom of Israel and Judah and that during the Kingdom of Judah, the temple was dedicated to Yahweh, and is said to have housed the Ark of the Covenant. Jewish historian Josephus says that "the temple was burnt four hundred and seventy years, six months, and ten days after it was built", although rabbinic sources state that the First Temple stood for 410 years and, based on the 2nd-century work Seder Olam Rabbah, place construction in 832 BC and destruction in 422 BC, 165 years later than secular estimates.

Because of the religious sensitivities involved, and the politically volatile situation in Jerusalem, only limited archaeological surveys of the Temple Mount have been conducted. No archaeological excavations have been allowed on the Temple Mount during modern times. Therefore, there are very few pieces of archaeological evidence for the existence of Solomon's Temple. An ivory pomegranate which mentions priests in the house "of — -h", and an inscription recording the Temple's restoration under Jehoash have both appeared on the antiquities market, but their authenticity has been challenged and they are the subject of controversy

https://en.wikipedia.org/wiki/Solomon%27s_Temple

The crowning achievement of King Solomon's reign was the erection of a magnificent temple in Jerusalem, often called Solomon's temple or the first temple. Solomon's father, King David, had wanted to build a great temple for God a generation earlier, as a permanent resting place for the Ark of the Covenant which contained the Ten Commandments. However, God had forbidden him from doing so: "You will not build a House for my name for you are a man of battles and have shed blood" (1 Chronicles 28:3). Then Solomon began to build the house of the LORD in Jerusalem on Mount Moriah, where the Lord had appeared to his father David (2 Chronicles 3:1). This new, stationary temple would replace the portable tabernacle constructed during the wilderness wandering.

If Solomon reigned from 970 to 930 BC, then he began building the temple in 966 BC. A very interesting fact concerning the building of the temple was that there was no noise of the construction. The material was prepared before it was brought to the building site. The house, while it was being built, was built of stone prepared at the quarry, and there was neither hammer nor axe nor any iron tool heard in the house while it was being built (1 Kings 6:7). The Bible's description of Solomon's temple suggests that the inside ceiling was 180 feet long, 90 feet wide, and 50 feet high. The highest point on the temple that King Solomon built was 120 cubits tall (about 20 stories or about 207 feet). (1 Kings 6:1–38 and chapters 7—8) describe the construction and dedication of Solomon's temple.

Until the first temple was destroyed by the Babylonians some four hundred years later, in 586 BC, sacrifice was the predominant mode of divine service there. Seventy years later, a second temple was completed on the same site, and sacrifices again resumed. The book of Ezra chronicles the building of the second temple. During the first century, Herod greatly enlarged and expanded this temple, which became known as Herod's temple. It was destroyed by the Romans in AD 70, during the siege of Jerusalem. Only a small portion of the retaining wall remains to this day, known as "The Wailing Wall."

https://www.gotquestions.org/Solomon-first-temple.html

Zerubbabel's Temple

2. Zerubbabel's Temple, "The Second Temple in Jerusalem"

In 538 BC, Zerubbabel, the leader of the tribe of Judah, was part of the first wave of Jewish captives to return to Jerusalem (Ezra 1:1–2). The Persian king appointed Zerubbabel as governor of Judah (Haggai 1:1), and right away Zerubbabel began rebuilding the temple with the help of Joshua, the high priest (Ezra 3:2–3, 8).

The first temple, built by King Solomon, had been destroyed by the Babylonians in 587 BC (2 Kings 25:8–10).

It took Zerubbabel two years to rebuild the foundation of the temple. Then construction was delayed by Samaritan settlers whose friendly overtures masked a hidden hostility (Ezra 4:1–5). As a result of the opposition to the temple construction, Persia withdrew support for the project, and for seventeen years the temple sat unfinished (Ezra 4:21).

Finally, God sent the prophets Haggai and Zechariah to encourage and support Zerubbabel (Ezra 5:1–2), and the work on the second temple resumed. Four years later, in 515 BC, the temple was completed and dedicated with great fanfare (Ezra 6:16). The Jews also observed the Passover (Ezra 6:19). It's interesting that Zerubbabel is never mentioned in connection with the dedication ceremonies, nor is his name mentioned again after Ezra 5:1. For this reason, Zerubbabel's temple is often referred to simply as the "SECOND TEMPLE."

It is obvious that the Lord God was pleased with Zerubbabel's efforts in returning the captives to Jerusalem, in building the second temple, and in reestablishing the temple worship (Ezra 3:10). With God's prompting, Haggai gave Zerubbabel a special blessing: "On that day,' declares the LORD Almighty, 'I will take you, my servant Zerubbabel son of Shealtiel,' declares the LORD, 'and I will make you like my signet ring, for I have chosen you,' declares the LORD Almighty" (Haggai 2:23).

As the second temple was being built, there was a group of Jews in Jerusalem who were rather disappointed. Older Jews who recalled the size and grandeur of the first temple regarded Zerubbabel's temple as a poor substitute for the original. To their minds, it did not even begin to compare with the splendor of Solomon's temple. It was true that Zerubbabel's temple was built on a smaller scale and with much fewer resources. Also, Solomon's temple had housed the Ark of the Covenant, which was no longer in Israel's possession.

And at the first temple's dedication, the altar had been lit by fire from heaven, and the temple had been filled with the <u>Shekinah</u>; attendees at the second temple's dedication witnessed no such miracles. Even so, Haggai prophesied that the second temple would one day have a magnificence to outshine the glory of the first (Haggai 2:3–9). Haggai's word was fulfilled 500 years later when Jesus Christ arrived on the scene (Luke 2:22, 46; 19:45). Zerubbabel's temple was not as outwardly impressive as Solomon's, but it had a greater glory: The Messiah Himself walked the courts of the temple that Zerubbabel built.

https://www.gotquestions.org/Zerubbabel-second-temple.html

3. Herod's Temple, The (third) Renovation Temple of Zerubbabel

When David was king, he asked God if he could build a temple (1 Chronicles 17:1–15). God told him no, but he could gather materials for his son, Solomon, to build it (1 Chronicles 22:2–5). This temple was destroyed and ransacked by the Babylonians in 586 BC (2 Kings 25:9). King Darius allowed the temple to be rebuilt (Ezra 1:2), but construction was slow as those who returned from exile concentrated on the wall around Jerusalem and their own livelihoods. Over the next four hundred years, a series of Gentile rulers alternately built up and defiled the temple. The cycle culminated in the battle in 39 BC, in which Herod took control of the temple, slaughtering many of the priests and defenders, but kept the Roman soldiers from going into the sanctuary. Herod proposed to renovate the temple in 20-19 BC; his reason being the post-exilic temple was sixty cubits shorter than Solomon's original. Despite the Jews' fears that he meant to tear it down and forget to rebuild it, the main work on the temple was completed in one-and-a-half years and the outer courtyard in eight years. Finishing touches continued until AD 63.

On the eastern edge of Jerusalem, just west of Gethsemane and northwest of the Kidron Valley sat the Temple of Herod. Literature states that the outer walls formed a rough rectangle, 500 feet long by 100 feet wide, slightly narrower on the south than the north, and slightly tilted to the northwest. Archeological evidence, however, has the dimensions closer to 1,550 feet by 1000 feet. On the far northwest corner sat Antonia Fortress, the home of the temple garrison that stayed alert for disturbances in the temple—disturbances that could gain the governor unwanted attention from Rome.

Two gates provided entry into the temple court from the south, four from the west, one, the Golden Gate, from the east, and an underground passage led from Antonia Fortress. Just inside the walls ran porticoes—roofed walkways flanked on the outside by the great walls and the inside by rows of tall marble pillars. The northern entrance was the most level and easiest to climb, but the southern gates (the double Huldah and the triple Huldah) the most frequently used. Because a ravine lined the southern wall, great staircases led to the actual gates. Tunnels passed through and into a honeycombed underground area called "Solomon's Stable." More stairs led up to the southern section of the Court of the Gentiles. The eastern portico was named for King Solomon, and it was somewhere along this wall that the twelve-year old Jesus debated with the scholars (Luke 2:46). It's possible that the highest corner of the eastern wall was where Satan took Jesus in Matthew 4:5. But it was the east gate, called Shushan, HaKohan, or Golden, that Nehemiah 3:29 and Ezekiel 44:1–3 prophesied the Messiah would use. Jesus rode through this gate on a donkey colt in Luke 19:28–48. The western wall is all that remains of the temple. It's now called the Wailing Wall.

The third temple itself sat skewed in the center of the large courtyard so that its entrance might better face due east. A balustrade a low wall of stone posts and caps — surrounded it, defining the inner boundary of the Court of Gentiles. It was this courtyard, between the balustrade and the outer walls, where Gentiles could go to worship. It was also this court where Jesus drove out the money changers in Matthew 21:12. It was unlawful for any Gentile to go past the balustrade, an offense punishable by death, which the Roman leaders allowed the Jewish authorities to carry out. Paul was attacked by a mob of Asian Jews in Acts 21:27–32 because it was presumed he took a Gentile friend beyond this court and into the temple. The commander of the garrison in Fort Antonia intervened before the crowd could kill him.

Like the outer courtyard, the temple was enclosed by a wall on the outside; storage and work rooms as well as gate houses lined the inside. Fourteen steps up the east side of the Court of the Gentiles sat the main entrance, possibly called the Beautiful Gate, which led to the Women's Court, although women were required to use the gates on the north and south. To the left of the entrance sat thirteen trumpet-shaped containers for voluntary offerings. It was here that Jesus noticed the widow donating her last mite in Mark 12:41–44. Directly west of the Beautiful Gate and up fifteen steps were the Gate of Nicanor, where Mary brought the Baby Jesus at the time of His presentation. Through this gate was the Court of Israel where the ceremonially clean Jewish men could congregate. Four gates, two on the south, two on the north, also led into this court. A low balustrade and another staircase separated it from the Court of the Priests; three gates, one each from the south, west, and north, provided direct access for the priests from the outer courtyard.

The center, near edge of the Court of Priests was dedicated to the altar. Forty-five feet on each side and twenty-two feet high, it was made of un-carved stone. In an earlier manifestation, the nearby area where the animals were slaughtered was fitted with a trough of running water, fed by a spring and underground cistern to wash away the blood. It's possible this was retained in Herod's version. Behind the altar sat the large laver resting on twelve bronze bulls, where the priests washed, and then yet another staircase leading to an embroidered curtain which hid away the temple. The temple was situated such that a priest burning a heifer on the top of the Mount of Olives could look over the short eastern wall, down the line past the Beautiful Gate and the Gate of Nicanor, and onto the entrance to the Holy Place.

The temple itself was set up similarly to the tabernacle of Moses. Beyond the first veil was the Hall which contained the Golden Altar for the incense offering, the Golden Table for the showbread, and the Golden Lampstand. It was this lampstand, the seven-armed menorah, which was said to have stayed lit during the eight-day rededication of the temple during the Maccabean Revolt in the second century BC, despite having only one day's worth of oil. Only priests could enter this area, and only the high priest, once a year, could go beyond the final veil to the Holy of Holies. Because the Ark of the Covenant had been lost years before, the room had no furnishings, although it is possible a stone held the place of the ark. It was this veil, into the Holy of Holies, which tore from the top down when Jesus was, crucified (Matthew 27:51). Around the Holy of Holies, to the south, west, and north were three stories of interconnected rooms. Openings from the upper story allowed workers to be lowered down and make repairs to the structure of the room without touching the ground.

The Romans were generally content to provide services and political stability to those they ruled in return for relative peace. The kings and governors they placed over Israel knew this, but in their greed and cultural unawareness (or apathy), they managed to frequently insult the Jews. Several times the local Roman authorities quelled riots and protests with massacres. After a long, destructive civil war between the Jewish Zealots and the Roman authorities, four legions, led by Titus the Roman general, besieged Jerusalem and burned down the temple in AD 70. As the temple burned, the gold and silver ornamentation melted and seeped between the cracks in the stones. In their zeal for a stipend, the Roman soldiers took the temple apart, stone by stone, fulfilling Jesus' prophecy in Matthew 24:1–3. The Jewish people were scattered in the Diaspora and did not return to Palestine until after World War II.

The Temple Mount, where Herod's temple stood, is now home to the Islamic mosque the Dome of the Rock. The Wailing Wall stands to the southwest of the mosque and north of an Islamic museum. The temple will not be rebuilt until the end times.

https://www.gotquestions.org/Herod-third-temple.html

Now that we have talked about the Jewish Temple, let's see the Muslims shrine which occupies the contentious center of the Holy side in Jerusalem.

The Temple of God – Revelation 11:1-2

This temple referred to in Revelation 11:1-2 is not Herod's renovated temple for that one was destroyed 70 AD some twenty five years before Revelation was written. Again, this temple can't be the Millennial temple as in Ezekiel 40-48, because it will not be built until Christ comes to Earth (Zechariah 6:12-13). This one is to be rebuilt by the Jews before Daniel's 70th Week. It will be destroyed at the end of the Tribulation, either by the earthquake under the seventh vail (Revelation 16:18-19) or by the armies of Anti-Christ at the taking of Jerusalem (Zechariah 14:1-). Both the Old and New Testaments are clear that there is to be such a temple where sacrifice will be offered for 3 ½ years. Then this temple will be made desolate for 3 ½ years and will be polluted by the Antichrist and the Gentiles (Daniel 9:27; 12:7-12; Matthew 24:15; 2 Thessalonians 2:2-4).

This treading down of Jerusalem by the Gentiles during the 42 months proves that the "Times of the Gentiles" will not end until the return of Christ at the end of 42 months. Luke 21:24 records it thus: "They will fall by the edge of the sword and be led captive among all nations, and Jerusalem will be trampled underfoot by the Gentile, until the times of the Gentiles are fulfilled."

4. The Dome of the Rock

The Dome of the Rock is a Muslim shrine that was completed on the Temple Mount in Jerusalem in AD 691. The Dome of the Rock is part of a larger Muslim holy area that takes up a significant portion of what is also known as Mount Moriah in the heart of Jerusalem. The Dome of the Rock gets its name from the fact that it is built over the highest part (the dome) of Mount Moriah which is where Jews and Christians believe Abraham was prepared to offer his son Isaac as a sacrifice to God (Genesis 22:1–14).

It is also considered to be the location of the threshing floor of Araunah, the Jebusite, where David built an altar to the Lord (2 Samuel 24:18). It is also on or very near the site that Herod's Temple stood before it was destroyed in AD 70 by the Roman army. Some even believe the rock might have been the location of the Holy of Holies that was a part of the Jewish Temple where the Jewish High Priest would enter once a year to make atonement for Israel's sins.

The Dome of the Rock is part of the larger Islamic area known as the Noble Sanctuary or Al-Haram al-Sharif. This area includes over 35 acres and contains both the Al-Aqsa Mosque and the Dome of the Rock. After Muslims took control of Jerusalem in AD 637, Islamic leaders commissioned the building of the Dome of the Rock in AD 685. It took almost seven years to complete and today is one of the world's oldest Islamic structures.

The platform or Temple Mount area that houses the Dome of the Rock and Al-Aqsa Mosque was built in the first century AD under the rule of Herod the Great as part of his rebuilding of the second Jewish Temple. Jesus worshiped at Herod's Temple and it was there that He prophesied its destruction (Matthew 24:1–2). Jesus' prophecy was fulfilled when the temple was destroyed by the Roman army in AD 70.

The Temple Mount area where the Dome of the Rock is located is important to not only the Muslims who control it now, but also to Jews and Christians. As the place where the Jewish temple once stood, the Temple Mount is the holiest place in Judaism and is the place where Jews and some Christians believe that the third and final temple will be built. This area is also the third holiest site in Islam. Because of its importance to both Jews and Muslims, the Temple Mount area is a highly contested religious site over which both the Palestinian Authority and Israel claim sovereignty.

The Dome of the Rock is an impressive structure, easily seen in many photographs of Jerusalem. Not only is it on top of Mount Moriah, but it was also built on an elevated platform raising it up another 16 feet above the rest of the Temple Mount area. Inside at the center of the Dome is the highest point of Mount Moriah. This bare rock measures about 60 feet by 40 feet and rises about 6 feet from the floor of the shrine. While many people mistakenly refer to the Dome of Rock as a mosque, it was built as a shrine for pilgrims, although it is located near the Al-Aqsa mosque.

Some believe the Dome of the Rock was built because, according to Muslim legend, the Prophet Muhammad was taken to Mount Moriah by the angel Gabriel, and from there Muhammad ascended into heaven and met all the prophets that had preceded him, as well as seeing God sitting on His throne surrounded by angels. However, this story does not appear in any Islamic texts until several decades after the shrine was built, which leads some to believe the primary reason the Dome was built was to celebrate the Islamic victory over Christians at Jerusalem and not to honor the supposed ascension of Muhammad.

When Israel took control over that part of Jerusalem after the Six-Day War in 1967, Israeli leaders allowed an Islamic religious trust to have authority over the Temple Mount and the Dome of the Rock as a way of helping keep the peace. Since that time non-Muslims have been allowed limited access to the area but are not permitted to pray on the Temple Mount.

https://www.gotquestions.org/Dome-of-the-Rock.html

Dome of the Rock

What is the Meaning and Significance of the Temple Mount?

1. The Temple Mount is the holiest site in Judaism, the third holiest site in Islam, and a revered site to Christians. To the Jews it is known as Har HaMoriyah ("Mount Moriah") and Har HaBayit ("Temple Mount"); to Muslims it is known as Haram el Sharif ("the Sacred Noble Sanctuary"). In the Bible it is also called Mount Zion (Psalm 48:2; Isaiah 4:5). Because of its importance to three major religions, its ownership has been hotly contested for nearly two thousand years. Today the Temple Mount is under the control

of the Jerusalem Islamic Waqf, a trust that was established in 1187 to manage the Islamic structures in Jerusalem. Under their current rules, access to the holy sites is prohibited to all non-Muslims.

According to the Bible (Genesis 22:1–14), God told Abraham to bring his son Isaac to the land of Moriah (meaning "Chosen by Yah") and offer him as a sacrifice on a mountain there. As Abraham was about to complete the sacrifice, God stopped him and provided a ram as a substitutionary sacrifice. In this same location, nearly 1,000 years later, God led Solomon to build the First Temple (2 Chronicles 3:1). David had identified this location as the place for worshiping God because it was here the plague was stayed when he confessed his sin, and he purchased the place, so he could build an altar (1 Chronicles 21:18–26). Solomon's Temple stood until the Babylonians destroyed it in 586 BC. Zerubbabel led the efforts to build the Second Temple, which was completed in 516 BC, then enlarged by Herod the Great in 12 BC. The Second Temple was destroyed by the Romans in AD 70, fulfilling Jesus' words in Mark 13:1–2.

As the Roman Empire was fading, Mohammed and his teaching of Islam was rising in the Middle East. According to the Quran (Surah 17:1), Mohammed made a miraculous night journey from Mecca to Jerusalem in AD 621. There he led worship at "the farthest mosque," was lifted to heaven, and returned to earth to carry on his teachings. At that time there was no mosque in Jerusalem, but 15 years later, Caliph Umar built a small mosque to commemorate the prophet's night visit. The Al Aqsa Mosque ("the farthest mosque") was built in AD 705, then rebuilt in 754, 780, and 1035. The Dome of the Rock was built in AD 692 over the place where Mohammad supposedly ascended to heaven. This rock is also identified by Christians and Jews as the place where Abraham offered Isaac and the location of the Holy of Holies in the Jewish temple. During the Crusades, Christians took temporary control of the Temple Mount, and the Al Aqsa Mosque was used as a palace and church in 1099.

The Temple Mount continues to be the center of controversy today. Though they are barred from entering the Muslim areas, Jews pray at the Western Wall (also known as the Wailing Wall), part of the remaining structure of the Temple Mount from the time of the Second Temple. The Islamic Waqf has created controversy with their decision to allow major renovations to the underground areas of the Temple Mount without regard to archaeological artifacts. Huge loads of earth have been removed from the area and dumped elsewhere. Archaeologists sifting through the dumped earth have recovered several artifacts of Jewish origin, though nothing that can be directly tied to the Jewish temple. Many Jews are preparing for the Third Temple to be built on the site, and Christians also look with interest on those preparations.

2. The Bible mentions that some end-times events will occur in a temple in Jerusalem (Daniel 9:27; Matthew 24:15). In 2 Thessalonians 2:4, Paul, speaking of the Antichrist, "who opposes and exalts himself against every so called god or object of worship, so that he takes his seat in the temple of God, proclaiming himself to be God." The Prophet Ezekiel described a temple that has yet never existed (Ezekiel chapters 40-48). Before the end times can occur, a temple must be present for these events to occur in.

There is still the "small" problem of the Islamic Dome of the Rock mosque being on the site where the Jewish temple is supposed to be. Muslims believe this is the place from which Mohammed ascended into heaven, making it the most sacred of Muslim shrines. For the Jews to take over this place and build a temple upon it would be unthinkable in today's political climate. But during the tribulation, the building of the Temple will come about, protected by the Antichrist (Daniel 9:24-27).

When we see the Temple being constructed, we can be sure the end times are indeed upon us. The Antichrist will be reigning, the Church will already have been raptured, and the first half of the tribulation will have passed

https://www.gotquestions.org/temple-mount.html

5. The Temple Institute of Jerusalem

The Temple Institute (in Hebrew, Machon HaMikdash), founded in 1987, is a Non-Profit Educational, and Religious Organization located in the Jewish quarter of Jerusalem's Old City. One of the Organization key aims is to educate Jews about the centrality of the Temple to Judaism, after nearly 2,000 years without it.

The Temple Institute is dedicated to every aspect of the holy temple of Jerusalem, and the central role it fulfilled, and will once again fulfill, in the spiritual wellbeing of both Israel and all the nations of the world. The Institute's work touches upon the history of the holy temple's past, an understanding of the present day, and the divine promise of Israel's future. The Institute's activities include education, research, and development. The Temple Institute's goal is to see Israel rebuild the holy temple on mount Moriah in Jerusalem, in accord with the biblical commandments

Architectural plans for The Third Temple have begun. While most Jews mourn and pray, one organization has been busily preparing plans to rebuild.

The Institute is also dedicated to every aspect of the Biblical Commandment to build the Holy Temple of God on Mount Moriah in Jerusalem.

The Short Term Goal

Is to rekindle the flame of the hearts of mankind of the significant the rebuilding and reinforce the true worship of God through Education.

The Long Term Goal

The long-term goal is to bring about the Holy Temple in our time. Thus, the Institute efforts include raising public awareness about the Holy Temple, and the central role that it occupies in the spiritual life mankind.

Major Focus

The major focus of the Institute is its efforts toward the beginning of the actual rebuilding of the Holy Temple. Towards this end, the Institute has begun to restore and construct the sacred vessels for the service of the Holy Temple. The vessels, which God commanded Israel to create, can be seen today at Institute's exhibition in Jerusalem's old city Jewish Quarter. "All the vessels of the tabernacle in all the service thereof, and the pins thereof, and all the pins of the court, shall de of brass" (Exodus 27:19 KJV) See also 1 Kings 10:27.

The Three Most Important Vessels

They are made according to the exact specifications of the Bible and have been constructed from the original source materials. Over 70 vessels have been recreated as at now for service and use in the third Holy Temple.

After many years of efforts, the institute has completed the most central vessels of the Divine service.

- **The Seven-Branched candelabra, or The Golden Menorah**, made of pure gold. (Exodus 25:31-40; 37:17-29), describe in detail in the above scriptures, stands along the southern side of the Kodesh Sanctuary of the Holy Temple. The Seven lamps of the menorah are kindled every day by a Kohen (priest) as part of the daily Tamid service.

The Seven-Branched candelabra

The Golden Incense Altar

(Exodus 30:1-10; 40:1)

The golden altar of incense, which is not to be confused with the brazen altar, sat in front of the curtain that separated the Holy Place from the Holy of Holies. This altar was smaller than the brazen altar. It was a square with each side measuring 1.5 feet and was 3 feet high. It was made of acacia wood and overlaid with pure gold. Four horns protruded from the four corners of the altar.

God commanded the priests to burn incense on the golden altar every morning and evening, the same time that the daily burnt offerings were made. The incense was to be left burning continually throughout the day and night as a pleasing aroma to the Lord. It was made of an equal part of four precious spices (stacte, onycha, galbanum and frankincense) and was considered holy. God commanded the Israelites not to use the same formula outside the tabernacle to make perfume for their own consumption; otherwise, they were to be cut off from their people (Exodus 30:34-38).

http://the-tabernacle place.com/articles/what_is_the_tabernacle/
tabernacle_altar_of_incense

https://www.templeinstitute.org/golden-incense-altar-gallery.htm

The Golden Table of the Showbread

(Exodus 25:23-30; Leviticus 24:5-7).

Now we will pass through the door of the tabernacle and enter the holy place. The priest had at his right hand the table of show-bread or also referred to as the table of the presence. It was made of acacia wood overlaid with pure gold. Its size was 2 cubits (3 feet) in length by one cubit (1 1/2 feet) in breadth and a height of 1 1/2 cubits (2 1/4 feet). Around the table was a border of gold and then a little further in, on the tabletop, an additional border which would hold the contents in place. The table had four legs, and two gold plated poles were inserted through golden rings attached to the legs for transporting.

The Institute has completed the sacred uniform of the Kohen Gadol of the High Priest. (Exodus 28) and the high priest's choshen breast-plate and ephod have been completed.

http://www.bible-history.com/tabernacle/TAB4The_Table_of_ Shewbread.htm

https://www.templeinstitute.org/

Conclusion

Jesus prophesied both the destruction of the temple and Jerusalem; therefore, it is necessary to discuss both prophecies to clearly understand the events that happened 40 years later.

"Jesus left the temple and was going away, when his disciples came to him to point out to him the buildings of the temple. But he answered them, 'You see all these, do you not? Truly, I say to you, there will not be left here one stone upon another that shall not be thrown down'" (Matthew 24:1-2).

The fulfillment of Christ's prophecy concerning the destruction of the magnificent temple at Jerusalem not only reveals the year of Christ's crucifixion, but also ended one phase of God's plan for the salvation of humanity and ushered in the next phase Christ's return to conquer and rule the earth.

In 40 BC, the Roman senate appointed Herod, later known as Herod the Great, as the ruler of Judea. Herod had previously served as the governor of Galilee and was a friend of Mark Antony before Antony was defeated by Octavian. Later Herod became a friend of Octavian who became the first Roman emperor as Caesar Augustus.

Herod the Great ruled Judea for the next 36 years, during which time he began many huge building projects including the building of a new Temple in Jerusalem for the worship of God. From the beginning of the Temple project in 19 BC, it took 46 years to complete the main building and another 36 years to finish the entire Temple complex. This was a huge undertaking which required a tremendous amount of labor and money. This new temple was said to be a larger and a more beautiful temple than the one that Solomon built.

The historian Josephus said that much of the exterior of the Temple was covered with gold that reflected the fiery rays of the sun. Moreover, he said that, from a distance, the Temple appeared like a mountain covered with snow. This was probably because those parts that were not covered with gold were made of white stone.

From what is said in many writings about Herod's Temple, it was indeed a magnificent structure of awesome proportions. However, four years after its completion, it was destroyed and wiped from the face of the earth.

During Jesus' time, many of the Jews were so awe struck and impressed with the grandeur of the Temple that they replaced the worship of God with respect and reverence for the Temple complex itself. However, Jesus was not impressed with the Temple's physical structure, because he knew that the Sovereign God was greater than any building that man could construct, no matter how grand and beautiful it was.

3

Three Categories of People

The scriptures teach that there are three separate classes or categories of people living on earth. "And what you have heard from me in the presence of many witnesses entrust these to faithful men, who will be able to teach others also." (2 Timothy 2:2) You see we must teach others out of their ignorance and unbelief. You can't love them out of their ignorance. The reason many are confused is because, we are not able to distinguish between times, and the types of people on earth. I am not talking about colors.

We meet them, chat with them and can identify these categories of people in our daily movement. They are: 1. The Jews, 2. The Gentiles and, 3. The Church. It is important to know and understand the background of each of the three categories and to know which one does each of us belong to as a person. You simply can't put the three together, you belong to one class or another, you just need to distinguish them, and know physically as people, who they each are. What does each category stand for, and what are their traits?

Category One–The Jews

The Jews are the first category of people God choose and started dealing with as a nation on earth after the generation of Noah. They were the Chosen nation. God first called them through Abraham out from Ur of the land of the Chaldees.

"And Terah took Abram his son, and Lot the son of Haran his son's son, and Sarai his daughter in law, his son Abram's wife; and they went forth with them from Ur of the Chaldees, to go into the land of Canaan; and they came unto Haran and dwelt there. And the days of Terah were two hundred and five years: and Terah died in Haran." (Genesis 11:31-32 KJV)

"Now the Lord had said unto Abram, get thee out of thy country, and from thy kindred, and from thy father's house, unto a land that I will shew thee: And I will make of thee a great nation, and I will bless thee, and make thy name great; and thou shalt be a blessing: And I will bless them that bless thee and curse him that curseth thee: and in thee shall all families of the earth be blessed. So, Abram departed, as the Lord had spoken unto him; and Lot went with him: and Abram was seventy and five years old when he departed out of Haran." (Genesis 12:1-4 KJV)

God embedded all three categories of people in Abraham, when He said "and in you all the families of the earth shall blessed. (Verse 3b) All the families include the Jews, the Gentiles and the Church. The Abrahamic blessing is universal

History of the Name Jews

The name Jew is primarily tribal from Judah and was never at first used among Israelites in the Bible until its first mention in 2 Kings 16:6 and 2 Kings 25:25.

> "At that time Rezin king of Syria recovered Elath to Syria, and drove the Jews from Elath, and the Syrians came to Elath and dwelt there unto this day." (2 Kings 16:6 KJV)

> "But in the seventh month, Ishmael the son of Nathanial, son of Elishama, of the royal family, came with ten men and struck down Gedaliah

and put him to death along with the Jews and the Chaldeans who were with him at Mizpah." (2 Kings 25:25 KJV)

After the captivity it was commonly used to distinguish the race of Israel from Gentiles. In those references the Hebrew word could have been better translated as "men of Judah", the word Jews is much more commonplace in the books of Ezra, Nehemiah, and Esther.

The usage of the word Jew in those books help explain the origin of the word and why it was used. Originally, God's chosen people were known as Hebrews, later after they settled in the Promised Land and formed a nation, they were known as the Israelites. The term "Jew" did not come into use until after the ten Northern tribes were exiled to Assyria and Judah was exiled to Babylon. However, Jews are simply the physical and direct descendants of Abraham, Isaac and Jacob that live on the land of Palestine today. You can't physically claim you are a Jew without been a direct blood line from Abraham, Isaac and Jacob.

Why is Israel a Chosen Nation?

Speaking of the nation of Israel, Deuteronomy 7:7-9 tells us, "The LORD did not set His affection on you and choose you because you were more numerous than other peoples, for you were the fewest of all peoples. But it was because the LORD loved you and kept the oath, He swore to your forefathers that He brought you out with a mighty hand and redeemed you from the land of slavery, from the power of Pharaoh king of Egypt. Know therefore that the LORD your God is God; He is the faithful God, keeping His covenant of love to a thousand generations of those who love Him and keep His commands."

God chose the nation of Israel to be the people through whom Jesus Christ would be born the Savior from sin and death (John 3:16).

God first promised the Messiah after Adam and Eve's fall into sin–Genesis 3:15: "And I will put enmity between thee and the woman, and between thy seed and her seed; it shall bruise thy head, and thou shalt bruise his heel)." God later confirmed that the Messiah would come from the line of Abraham, Isaac, and Jacob (Genesis 12:1-3). Jesus Christ is the ultimate reason why God chose Israel to be His special people. God did not need to have a chosen people, but He decided to do it that way. Jesus had to come from some nation of people, and God chose Israel.

However, God's reason for choosing the nation of Israel was not solely for producing the Messiah. God's desire for Israel was that they would go and teach others about Him. Israel was to be a nation of priests, prophets, and missionaries to the world. God's intent was for Israel to be a distinct people, a nation who pointed others towards God and His promised provision of a Redeemer, Messiah, and Savior. For the most part, Israel failed in this task. However, God's ultimate purpose for Israel that of bringing the Messiah into the world was fulfilled perfectly in the Person of Jesus Christ.

Category Two–The Gentiles

The word Gentile is an English translation of the Hebrew word Goyin, translated as heathen, non-Israelite or foreigner, nation, or group of people. "By these were the isles of the Gentiles divided in their lands, everyone after his tongue, after their lands, everyone after their nation" (Genesis 10:5 KJV).

From the Jewish perspective, Gentiles were often seen as pagans who did not know the true God. During Jesus time, many Jews took such pride in their cultural and religious heritage that they consider Gentiles "unclean" calling them "dogs" and uncircumcision.

It was even a taboo for a Gentile to go into the temple of the Jews to worship. They were only restricted to the courts. In the book of

Acts, chapter 21 we read how they nearly killed Paul for bringing a Gentile to the Temple.

Paul Is Arrested

"So Paul went to the Temple the next day with the other men. They had already started the purification ritual, so he publicly announced the date when their vows would end, and sacrifices would be offered for each of them. The seven days were almost ended when some Jews from the province of Asia saw Paul in the Temple and roused a mob against him. They grabbed him, yelling, "Men of Israel, help us! This is the man who preaches against our people everywhere and tells everybody to disobey the Jewish laws. He speaks against the Temple—and even defiles this holy place by bringing in Gentiles." (For earlier that day they had seen him in the city with Trophimus, a Gentile from Ephesus, and they assumed Paul had taken him into the Temple.)

The whole city was rocked by these accusations, and a great riot followed. Paul was grabbed and dragged out of the Temple, and immediately the gates were closed behind him. As they were trying to kill him, word reached the commander of the Roman regiment that all Jerusalem was in an uproar. He immediately called out his soldiers and officers and ran down among the crowd. When the mob saw the commander and the troops coming, they stopped beating Paul.

Then the commander arrested him and ordered him bound with two chains. He asked the crowd who he was and what he had done. Some shouted one thing and some another. Since he couldn't find out the truth in all the uproar and confusion, he ordered that Paul be taken to the fortress. As Paul reached the stairs, the mob grew so violent the soldiers had to lift him to their shoulders to protect him. And the crowd followed behind, shouting, "Kill him, kill him!"

Paul Speaks to the Crowd

As Paul was about to be taken inside, he said to the commander, "May I have a word with you?" "Do you know Greek?" the commander asked, surprised. "Aren't you the Egyptian who led a rebellion some time ago and took 4,000 members of the Assassins out into the desert?"

"No," Paul replied, "I am a Jew and a citizen of Tarsus in Cilicia, which is an important city. Please, let me talk to these people." The commander agreed, so Paul stood on the stairs and motioned to the people to be quiet. Soon a deep silence enveloped the crowd, and he addressed them in their own language, Aramaic." (Acts 21:26-40 NLT)

Gentiles and the Half-Gentiles

Samaritans are the Gentiles and Half-Gentiles because they were people who live in what had been the Northern kingdom of Israel.

> "And the king of Assyria brought people from Babylon, Cuthah, Avva, Hamath, and Sepharvaim, and placed them in the cities of Samaria instead of the people of Israel. And they took possession of Samaria and lived in its cities. And at the beginning of their dwelling there, they did not fear the LORD. Therefore, the LORD sent lions among them, which killed some of them. So, the king of Assyria was told, "The nations that you have carried away and placed in the cities of Samaria do not know the law of the god of the land. Therefore, he has sent lions among them, and behold, they are killing them, because they do not know the law of the god of the land." Then the king of Assyria commanded, "Send there one of the priests whom you carried away from there and let him go and dwell there and

teach them the law of the god of the land." So, one of the priests whom they had carried away from Samaria came and lived in Bethel and taught them how they should fear the LORD." (2 Kings 17:24-28)

The descendants of these foreigners and the remnant of Israel were simply called "Samaritans". During the time of Christ, the Samaritans were despised as an "Unclean" people because of their mixed ancestry and rejection of Temple-based worship.

Samaritans were viewed as enemies to be shunned (John 4:9; 18:28; Acts 10:28). In the Sermon on the Mount, Jesus alluded to the common association of Gentiles with paganism: "if you greet only your brothers, what more are you doing than others? Do not even the Gentiles do the same? (Matthew 5:47). In another place in the same sermon, Jesus noted: "and when you pray do not heap up empty phrases as the Gentiles do, for they think they will be heard for their many words." (Matthew 6:7). In both cases, the NIV translates the word "Gentile" in question as "Pagan".

Jesus came to offer Salvation to all people, Jews and Gentiles. "For God so loved the world, that he gave his only Son, that whoever believes in him should not perish but have eternal life". (John 3:16) The prophet Isaiah predicted the Messiah's worldwide ministry, saying "He will bring justice to the Gentiles" and "would be a light to the Gentiles" (Isaiah 42:1, 6 NKJV).

The Syrophoenician Woman's Faith

Jesus helps a Gentile woman who had asked for her daughter's freedom from a demon:

> "And from there he arose and went away to the region of Tyrel and Sidon. And he entered a house and did not want anyone to know, yet he could not be hidden. But immediately a woman whose

little daughter had an unclean spirit heard of him and came and fell at his feet. Now the woman was a Gentile, a Syrophoenician by birth. And she begged him to cast the demon out of her daughter." (Mark 7:24-26)

Category Three–The Church

The Origin of the Church

Jesus Prophesied the building of His Church

"And I tell you, you are Peter, and on this rock, I will build my church, and the gates of hell shall not prevail against it. I will give you the keys of the kingdom of heaven, and whatever you bind on earth shall be bound in heaven, and whatever you lose on earth shall be loosed in heaven." (Matthew 16:18-19)

"Therefore, a man shall leave his father and mother and hold fast to his wife, and the two shall become one flesh." This mystery is profound, and I am saying it refers to Christ and the church". (Ephesians 5:31-32)

The Church is the: "The mystery hidden for ages and generations but now revealed to his saints". (Colossians 1:26). Numerous prophecies said in the past, but none was about the church. She is God's mystery revealed in our days.

It's important to note that when Jesus spoke of building His church, He was not referring to a literal building. The word church has become synonymous with a building or institution, and we have lost sight of the original meaning as written in Greek of "ekklhsia" which means the body or company of believers in Christ; the community of Christians on earth or saints in heaven, or both.

Although the establishment of the church followed after Jesus ascension, He was already advising how it should adjudicate grievances and disputes, when a brother sin against another. (Matthew 18:17)

Amongst the first references to the church are these in the Book of Acts:

> "And the Lord added to the church daily those who were being saved." (Acts 2:47 NKJV)

> "And great fear came upon the whole church and upon all who heard these things." (Acts 5:11 NKJV)

And it did not take long before persecution of the church is recorded, most notoriously at the hands of Saul who became Paul:

> "Now Saul was consenting to his [Stephen's] death. At that time a great persecution arose against the church which was at Jerusalem; and they were all scattered throughout the regions of Judea and Samaria, except the apostles." (Acts 8:1 NKJV)

> "As for Saul, he made havoc of the Church, entering every house, and dragging off men and women, committing them to prison." (Acts 8:3 NKJV)

By Acts chapter 11 we see the first mention of church and Christian together:

> "So it was that for a whole year they [Barnabas and Paul] assembled with the church and taught a great many people. And the disciples were first called Christians in Antioch." (Acts 11:26 NKJV)

The Purpose of the Church

The Purpose of the Church is to bring in and join people from different backgrounds, gifts and talents, to equip and provide for them, opportunities for God's work and salvation through our Lord Jesus Christ. It accomplishes this internally, within the body and externally in the world. Jesus gave us the vision for the church's primary focus:

> "And Jesus came and said to them, "All authority in heaven and on earth has been given to me. Go therefore and make disciples of all nations, baptizing them in the name of the Father and of the Son and of the Holy Spirit, teaching them to observe all that I have commanded you. And behold, I am with you always, to the end of the age." (Matthew 28:18-20)

The parallel passage from Mark:

> "And he said to them, "Go into the entire world and proclaim the gospel to the whole creation. Whoever believes and is baptized will be saved, but whoever does not believe will be condemned. (Mark 16:15-16)

We can't love people out from unbelief and out of little faith, but we can teach people out of their unbelief to grow to become who they are. As God choose Israel to teach other nations about Him, so Christians have been choosing to go out to preach the Gospel of Jesus Christ to whole world.

A. Internally

If Jesus provided the vision, acts 2:42 can be considered a purpose statement for the church: "And they devoted themselves to the apostles' teaching and the fellowship, to the breaking of bread and the prayers."

According to this verse, the purposes/activities of the church should be:

1) Apostolic teaching & biblical doctrine,
2) Providing a place of fellowship for believers,
3) Partaking of the Lord's Supper, and
4) Praying.

1. Apostolic Teaching & Biblical Doctrine

The phrase comes from Acts 2:42 quoted above.

The apostles taught the truth about Jesus Christ and the Gospel. They taught about the way in which he fulfilled the Old Testament Scriptures to bring people to salvation through His sacrificial death on the cross and His resurrection. They reaffirmed their witness to the events themselves, (Luke 24:48, Acts 2:32 and Acts 3:15). They also taught how salvation in Jesus Christ was to be worked out in the life of the believer. (Romans 1:5) They were not teaching something that they have made up in their own minds, but only things which have been revealed to them by Jesus and the Holy Spirit, and to which they had personal witness testimony. Jesus had already made it clear to them that their teaching was to be consistent with His: "So Jesus said to the Jews who had believed him, "If you abide in my word, you are truly my disciples." (John 8:31)

These teachings are revealed to us in the New Testament Scriptures. Some of the New Testament books are written by apostles themselves (Matthew, John, Peter and Paul), so they are obviously 'the apostles' teaching'. However, the others are written by their associates (Mark, Luke, James and Jude), not the apostles themselves, and for one book, the letter we call Hebrews, the author is not even known. The reason why these writings are included in the New Testament is because 'who wrote this?' is not the most important question to answer. The most important question is "Is this consistent with the apostles' teaching?" When you read Hebrews and any of the other books of the New Testament, you realize that this is clearly the case.

So, we use the terms 'apostles' teaching' or 'apostles' doctrine' as a shorthand way of describing the true and consistent teaching of the New Testament. To apply this to ourselves, the most important question for us to ask when we hear people teach, or when we seek to teach others, is same question as before. "Is this consistent with the apostles' teaching?" We are not to deviate from the teaching of the apostles, as Paul says in his letter to the Thessalonians:

"But we ought always to give thanks to God for you, brothers beloved by the Lord, because God chose you as the first fruits to be saved, through sanctification of the Spirit and belief in the truth. To this He called you through our gospel, so that you may obtain the glory of our Lord Jesus Christ. So then, brothers, stand firm and hold to the traditions that you were taught by us, either by our spoken word or by our letter." (2 Thessalonians 2:13-15).

All teaching must be weighed to see if it is in line with that of the Scriptures. If it is, receive it with joy and put it into practice on your life. If it isn't, reject it and challenge it where appropriate by pointing to what the Bible says.

The church is to teach biblical doctrine, so we can be grounded in our faith. Ephesians 4:11-14 tells us:

> "And he gave the apostles, the prophets, the evangelists, the shepherds and teachers, to equip the saints for the work of ministry, for building up the body of Christ, until we all attain to the unity of the faith and of the knowledge of the Son of God, to mature manhood, to the measure of the stature of the fullness of Christ, so that we may no longer be children, tossed to and fro by the waves and carried about by every

wind of doctrine, by human cunning, by craftiness in deceitful schemes." (Ephesians 4:11-14)

To equip the church means teaching and developing the members to grow in the faith which was measured for them at the new birth in Christ. (For by the grace given to me I say to everyone among you not to think of himself more highly than he ought to think, but to think with sober judgment, each according to the measure of faith that God has assigned. Roman 12:3)

Sound Teaching is healthy and leads to building up the body of Christ. With sound doctrine, children of God are freed from satanic slavery and dominations.

https://wordatwork.org.uk/answers/ what-does-apostles-teaching-mean

Example Teaching Chart –

Dr. Better Serwa Ayi's Inspirational Teaching Chart

2. Fellowship

The church is to be a place of fellowship, where Christians can be devoted to one another in love and honor one another (Romans 12:10), instruct one another (Romans 15:14), be kind and compassionate to one another (Ephesians 4:32), encourage one another (1 Thessalonians 5:11; Hebrews 10:25), and most importantly, love one another (John 13:34 & 1 John 3:11).

In fellowship each member sees the reality of their hope in Christ Jesus. Two are always better than one, and how good it is for brethren to dwell together.

> "Two are better than one, because they have a good reward for their toil. For if they fall, one will lift his fellow. But woe to him who is alone when he falls and has not another to lift him up! Again, if two lies together, they keep warm, but how can one keep warm alone? And though a man might prevail against one who is alone, two will withstand him—a threefold cord is not quickly broken." (Ecclesiastes 4:9-12)

"I was glad when they said to me,
"Let us go to the house of the Lord."
And now here we are,
standing inside your gates, O Jerusalem.
Jerusalem is a well-built city;
its seamless walls cannot be breached.
All the tribes of Israel the Lord's people
make their pilgrimage here.
They come to give thanks to the name of the Lord,
as the law requires of Israel.
Here stand the thrones where judgment is given,
the thrones of the dynasty of David.
Pray for peace in Jerusalem.
May all who love this city prosper.

O Jerusalem may there be peace within your walls
and prosperity in your palaces.
For the sake of my family and friends, I will say,
"May you have peace."
For the sake of the house of the Lord our God, I will seek what is
best for you, O Jerusalem." (Psalm 122 NLV)

The Lord says He will seek what is best for us in fellowship.

3. Breaking of Bread

The church is to be a place where believers can observe the Lord's
Supper, remembering Christ's death and shed blood on our behalf
(1 Corinthians 11:23-26). The concept of "breaking bread" (Acts
2:42) also carries the idea of having meals together. This is another
example of the church promoting fellowship. The practice of the
Lord's Supper unifies us as it reminds us that we are all saved by
Christ's sacrificial work and then to proclaim his Salvation message to all mankind.

Practically, it also provides an opportunity to reconcile our differ-
ences of right and wrongs as we interacts with fellow believers.
(Matthew 18:17 and 1 Corinthians 11:27-28)

The breaking of bread is one of only two rituals, along with baptism by immersion that was commanded by our Lord Jesus Christ
to be practiced in the Church.

4. Prayers

The natural result of sound teaching is to unify the body of
Christ, that, the members of the Church will take care of one
another. The most powerful way to care for each other's is to
pray for the members of the Churches wellbeing daily, just as
the early Church prayed for each other.

> "And when he had seized him, he put him in
> prison, delivering him over to four squads of sol-
> diers to guard him, intending after the Passover
> to bring him out to the people. So, Peter was
> kept in prison, "but earnest prayer for him was
> made to God by the church". (Acts 12:4-5)

The church is to be a place that promotes prayer, teaches prayer, and practices prayer. In his letter to the Philippians Paul encourages us:

> "Do not be anxious about anything, but in every-
> thing, by prayer and supplication with thanksgiving,
> let your requests be made known to God. And the
> peace of God, which surpasses all understanding,
> will guard your hearts and your minds in Christ
> Jesus." (Philippians 4:6-7)

Prayer is the machinery that should always support the church.

B. External Purpose of the Church

Another commission given to the church is that of proclaiming the gospel of salvation through Jesus Christ (Matthew 28:18-20; Acts 1:8). The church is called to be faithful in sharing the gospel through word and in deed. The church is to be a "lighthouse" in the community, pointing people toward our Lord and Savior Jesus Christ. The church is to both promote the gospel and prepare its members to proclaim the gospel (1 Peter 3:15).

Some final purposes of the church are given in James 1:27: "Religion that God our Father accepts as pure and faultless is this: to look after orphans and widows in their distress and to keep one-self from being polluted by the world." The church is to be about the business of ministering to those in need. This includes not only sharing the gospel, but also providing for physical needs (food, clothing, shelter) as necessary and appropriate. This mirrors the ministry of our Lord who met physical needs of healing as proof of His authority to bring spiritual healing. The church is also to equip believers in Christ with the tools they need to overcome sin and remain free from the pollution of the world. This is done by biblical teaching and Christian fellowship.

So, what is the purpose of the church? Paul gave an excellent illustration to the believers in Corinth. The church is God's hands, mouth, and feet in this world, the body of Christ (1 Corinthians 12:12-27). We are to be doing the things that Jesus Christ would do if He were here physically on the earth. The church is to be "Christian," "Christ-like," and "Christ-following".

We the Church are described by Paul as ambassadors:

2 Corinthians 5:18-20:

> "And all of this is a gift from God, who brought us back to himself through Christ. And God has given us this task of reconciling people to him. For God was in Christ, reconciling the world to himself, no longer counting people's sins against them. And he gave us this wonderful message of reconciliation. So, we are Christ's ambassadors; God is making his appeal through us. We speak for Christ when we plead, "Come back to God!" (2 Corinthians 5:18-20 NLT)

4

The Beginning of Gentile Dominion Over Israel

I t all started with the Egyptians bondage: "Now there arose a new king over Egypt, who did not know Joseph. And he said to his people, "Behold, the people of Israel are too many and too mighty for us. Come, let us deal shrewdly with them, lest they multiply, and, if war breaks out, they join our enemies and fight against us and escape from the land." Therefore, they set taskmasters over them to afflict them with heavy burdens. They built for Pharaoh Store cities, Pithom and Rameses. (Exodus 1:8-11).

Followed by Assyria by Pul, in approximately 740 BC.

> "So the God of Israel stirred up the spirit of Pul king of Assyria, the spirit of Tilgath-pileser king of Assyria, and he took them into exile, namely, the Reubenites, the Gadites, and the half tribe of Manasseh, and brought them to Halah, Habor, Hara, and the river Gozan, to this day. (1 Chronicles 5:26)

The Assyrian captivity (or the Assyrian exile) is the period in the history of Ancient Israel and Judah during which several thousand Israelites of ancient Samaria were resettled as captives by Assyria. The Northern Kingdom of Israel was conquered by the Neo-Assyrian monarchs, Tiglath-Pileser III (Pul) and Shalmaneser

V. The later Assyrian rulers Sargon II and his son and successor, Sennacherib, were responsible for finishing the twenty-year demise of Israel's northern ten-tribe kingdom, although they did not over- take the Southern Kingdom. Jerusalem was besieged, but not taken. The tribes forcibly resettled by Assyria later became known as the Ten Lost Tribes. (1 Chronicles 5:23-26)

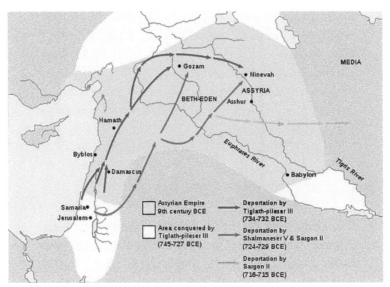

Deportation of the Northern Kingdom of Israel by the Assyrian Empire.

https://en.wikipedia.org/wiki/Assyrian_captivity

The record of 70 years of captivity of Israel from the book of Daniel:

"In the third year of the reign of Jehoiakim king of Judah, Nebuchadnezzar king of Babylon came to Jerusalem and besieged it. And the Lord gave Jehoiakim king of Judah into his hand, with some of the vessels of the house of God. And he brought them to the land of Shinar, to the house of his god, and placed the vessels in the treasury of his god. Then the king commanded Ashpenaz, his chief eunuch, to bring some of the people of Israel, both royal family and of the nobility, youths without blemish, of good appearance and skillful in all wisdom, endowed with knowledge, understanding learning, and competent to stand in the king's palace, and to teach them the literature and language of the Chaldeans. The king assigned them a daily portion of the food that the king ate, and of the wine that he drank. They were to be educated for three years, and at the end of that time they were to stand before the king. Among these were Daniel, Hananiah, Mishael, and Azariah of the tribe of Judah. And the chief of the eunuchs gave them names: Daniel he called Belteshazzar, Hananiah he called Shadrach, Mishael he called Meshach, and Azariah he called Abednego." (Daniel 1:1-5)

The prophet Jeremiah also refers to this period:

"For thus says the Lord: When seventy years are completed for Babylon, I will visit you, and I will fulfill to you my promise and bring you back to this place. For I know the plans I have for you, declares the Lord, plans for welfare and not for evil, to give you a future and a hope. Then you will call upon me and come and pray to me, and I will hear you. You will seek me and find me when you seek me with all your heart. I will be found by you, declares the Lord, and I will restore your fortunes and gather you from all the nations and all the places where I have driven you, declares the Lord, and I will bring you back to the place from which I sent you into exile." (Jeremiah 29:10-14)

It is in this account that began the Times of the Gentiles which was to continue through the 70 years of the great tribulation called "The time of Jacob's trouble" a phrase found nowhere else in Scripture than here:

"Alas! For that day is great, so that none is like it: it is even the time of Jacob's trouble; but he shall be saved out of it." (Jeremiah 30:7 KJV)

The Eight (8) Mountain Kingdom and Israel

I will now discuss further, the details of those Gentile Nations which dominated and oppressed Israel in the history of man.

1. The Egyptian Empire or the Chaldeans

The Egyptians were the first kingdom to oppress Israel in the times of the Gentiles, a period which spans Israel's history from the beginning as a nation in Egypt to the second advent of Jesus Christ.

"They will fall by the edge of the sword and be led captive among all nations, and Jerusalem will be trampled underfoot by the Gentiles, until the times of the Gentiles are fulfilled." (Luke 21:24)

"Lest you be wise in your own sight, I do not want you to be unaware of this mystery, brothers: a partial hardening has come upon Israel, until the fullness of the Gentiles has come in. And in this way all Israel will be saved, as it is written, "The Deliverer will come from Zion, he will banish ungodliness from Jacob"; (Romans 11:25-26)

"Then I was given a measuring rod like a staff, and I was told, "Rise and measure the temple of God and the altar and those who worship there, but do not measure the court outside the temple; leave that out, for it is given over to the nations, and they will trample the holy city for forty-two months." (Revelation 11:1-2)

God delivered the children of Israel by the leadership of Moses and established the great nation of Israel under King David and Solomon his son. Even until the Roman Empire days, Egypt was still Israel's bitter enemy, except for a few years' period of friendship.

Egypt was the place where Israel became a nation and where they were oppressed over 48 years, before Moses led them out of bondage.

> "Then the Lord said to him, "Know for certain that for four hundred years your descendants will be strangers in a country, that is not their own and that they will be enslaved and mistreated there. But I will punish the nation that enslaves them, and in the end, they will come away with great wealth."
> (Genesis 15:13-14 NLT)

Egypt is mentioned many times after this as the oppressor of Israel. She will be subject under the 8th kingdom in the book of Revelation. (Revelation 17:8-17; Daniel 8:21-25; 11:40-45) but Egypt will never be a great world power again.

> "It shall be the most lowly of the kingdoms, and never again exalt itself above the nations. And I will make them so small that they will never again rule over the nations." (Ezekiel 29:15)

What were Egyptian pharaohs doing in Bronze Age Jerusalem?

The archaeologist Gabriel Barkay investigated evidence of an Egyptian temple in Jerusalem, exposing the "Egyptianizing" of Bronze Age Jerusalem. Based on his work, in the March/April 2013 issue of BAR (www.biblicalarchaeology.org), Peter van der Veen presents new evidence of an Egyptian presence in Bronze

Age Jerusalem before David made the city the Israelite capital. In "When Pharaohs Ruled Jerusalem," Peter van der Veen brings together an array of evidence including Egyptian statues, stylized architecture and material culture that points to their presence in the city. But what did the Egyptian pharaohs want with Late Bronze Age Jerusalem? And where were they when David conquered the Jebusite city?

The initial study by Gabriel Barkay (which Peter van der Veen refers to as "reminiscent of nothing so much as Sherlock Holmes") exposed Egyptianizing column capitals, a hieroglyphic stela and two Egyptian-style alabaster vessels that likely served as burial gifts. Peter van der Veen expanded the investigations of Gabriel Barkay to include figurines and Egyptian statues as well as a funerary stela referring to the local "ruler" of Bronze Age Jerusalem.

The Egyptian artifacts date to the 13th century BC, during the 19th Egyptian Dynasty that included the reign of Ramesses II. Peter van der Veen writes, "Egypt was not new to Canaan in the 19th dynasty Canaan was in effect an Egyptian province during the 14th century BC." In the famous Amarna letters, Abdi-Heba, the puppet-king of Jerusalem, proclaims that "the king has placed his name in Jerusalem forever." While Bronze Age Jerusalem was not situated on Canaanite trade routes, Peter van der Veen notes that it controlled north-south traffic between Hebron and Shechem, as well as east-west traffic from the Via Maris to the King's Highway. The Egyptians established a garrison at Manahat, just two miles southwest of Bronze Age Jerusalem.

Bronze Age Jerusalem

Peter van der Veen augmented a study by Gabriel Barkay on the Egyptian pharaohs' rule over Bronze Age Jerusalem, uncovering Egyptian statues, architectural elements and texts attesting to their presence in the city. This 13th-century BC red granite statue depicts an Egyptian queen. The Egyptian statue's significance went unnoticed for quite some time; uncovered by Arab workmen during the British Mandate, it was brought to a local clergyman's house before being kept in a scholar's office in Germany. Credit: R. Müller, Department of Prehistory, University of Mainz.

https://www.biblicalarchaeology.org/daily/biblical-sites-places/jerusalem/when-egyptian-pharaohs-ruled-bronze-age-jerusalem/

2. The Assyrian Empire

The Assyrian empire is the second great Empire head of the beast to oppress Israel in the Times of the Gentiles.

It was founded by Nimrod:

> "Cush fathered Nimrod; he was the first on earth to be a mighty man. He was a mighty hunter before the Lord. Therefore it is said, "Like Nimrod a mighty hunter before the Lord." The beginning of his kingdom was Babel, Erech, Accad, and Calneh, in the land of Shinar. From that land he went into Assyria and built Nineveh, and the city Rehoboth-Ir, Calah, and Resen between Nineveh and Calah; that is the great city." (Genesis 10:8-12)

The Assyrian Empire was inferior to the Egyptian Empire.

The Assyrian Empire initiated Israelite's captivity by taking the ten northern tribes in 740 BC. These became the ten lost tribes of Israel.

> "Therefore, the LORD was very angry with Israel and removed them out of his sight. None was left but the tribe of Judah only. Judah also did not keep the commandments of the LORD their God but walked in the customs that Israel had introduced. And the LORD rejected all the descendants of Israel and afflicted them and gave them into the hand of plunderers, until he had cast them out of his sight. When he had torn Israel from the house of David, they made Jeroboam the son of Nebat king. And Jeroboam drove Israel from following the LORD and made them commit great sin. The people of Israel walked in all the sins that Jeroboam did. They did not depart from them, until the LORD removed Israel out of his sight, as he had spoken by all his servants

the prophets. So, Israel was exiled from their own land to Assyria until this day." (2 Kings 17:18-23)

When and How Was Israel Conquered by The Assyrians?

Assyrian's conquest of the northern kingdom began approximately 740 BC under King Pul.

> "So, the God of Israel stirred up the spirit of Pul king of Assyria, the spirit of Tiglath-Pileser king of Assyria, and he took them into exile, namely, the Reubenites, the Gadites, and the half-tribe of Manasseh, and brought them to Halah, Habor, Hara, and the river Gozan, to this day." (1 Chronicles 5:26)

These tribes; located east of the Jordan River, were the first ones conquered by Assyria. Nearly 20 years later in 722 BC, the capital city, Samaria, was overtaken by the Assyrians under Shahmaneser V. After first forcing tribute payments, Shahmaneser later laid siege to the city when Medes refused to pay, following a three year seiged. But the king of Assyria found treachery in Hoshea, for he had sent messengers to, king of Egypt, and offered no tribute to the king of Assyria, as he had done year by year. Therefore, the king of Assyria shut him up and bound him in prison. Then the king of Assyria invaded all the land and came to Samaria, and for three years he besieged it.

(A). The Fall of Samaria

> "But one-year Hoshea sent messengers to So, king of Egypt, asking for his help, and stopped paying the annual tribute to Assyria. When Shalmaneser learned of this, he had Hoshea arrested and put

in prison. Then Shalmaneser invaded Israel and besieged Samaria. In the third year of the siege, which was the ninth year of the reign of Hoshea, the Assyrian emperor captured Samaria, took the Israelites to Assyria as prisoners, and settled some of them in the city of Halah, some near the Habor River in the district of Gozan and some in the cities of Media." (2 Kings 17:4-6 [Good News Translation – GNT])

(B). The Fall of Israel

"In the ninth year of Hoshea, the king of Assyria captured Samaria, and he carried the Israelites away to Assyria and placed them in Halah, and on the Habor, the river of Gozan, and in the cities of the Medes." (2 Kings 17:6)

In 701 BC the Assyrians marched south into Judah, however they were unable to capture Jerusalem due the LORD's intervention.

"So, the LORD saved Hezekiah and the inhabitants of Jerusalem from the hands of Sennacherib king of Assyria. And He provided for them on every side." (2 Chronicles 32:22)

The Lord had long warned Israel of judgment, going all the way back to Moses stern warning (Deuteronomy 28:62-65; 2 Kings 17:13)

"Yet the LORD warned Israel and Judah by every prophet and every seer," (2 Kings 17:13a)

Many attempts had been made to turn the people back to the LORD, including efforts by Elijah and Elisha, two of the greatest prophets in Israel's history.

3. Babylonian Empire

Babylon was the third Empire to oppress Israel in the Times of the Gentiles. It is the first one mentioned in the book of Daniel, and for that reason many teachers of the Bible start the Times of the Gentiles with Babylon. It was during this period, when Israel was in total captivity in Babylon by Nebuchadnezzar. (2 King 25:1-26; Jeremiah 25)

Daniel foresaw them in his days, while John in Revelation saw the whole length of the Times of the Gentiles from Egypt to the Revived Greece Empire in the future. The purpose of being to identify the 8th Kingdom that will complete the Times of the Gentiles that Jesus Christ here spoke about.

> "They will fall by the edge of the sword and be led captive among all nations, and Jerusalem will be trampled underfoot by the Gentiles, until the times of the Gentiles are fulfilled." (Luke 21:24)

> "Therefore, the Lord brought upon them the commanders of the army of the king of Assyria, who captured Manasseh with hooks and bound him with chains of bronze and brought him to Babylon." (2 Chronicles 33:11)

> "And the king of Assyria brought people from Babylon, Cuthah, Avva, Hamath, and Sepharvaim, and placed them in the cities of Samaria instead of the people of Israel. And they took possession of Samaria and lived in its cities. And at the beginning of their dwelling there, they did not fear nor know the Lord. Therefore, the Lord sent lions among them, which killed some of them. So, the king of Assyria was told, "The nations that you have carried away and placed in the cities of Samaria do not know the law of the god of the land. Therefore,

he has sent lions among them, and behold, they are killing them, because they do not know the law of the god of the land." Then the king of Assyria commanded, "Send there one of the priests whom you carried away from there and let him go and dwell there and teach them the law of the god of the land." So, one of the priests whom they had carried away from Samaria came and lived in Bethel and taught them how they should fear the Lord. But every nation still made gods of its own and put them in the shrines of the high places that the Samaritans had made, every nation in the cities in which they lived. The men of Babylon made Succoth-benoth, the men of Cuth made Nergal, the men of Hamath made Ashima." (2 Kings 17:24-30)

And Babylon was chosen of God to take Judah captive for 70 years. She is mentioned under the head of gold:

"You O king are a king of kings. For the God of heaven has given you a kingdom, power, strength, and glory and wherever the children of men dwell, or the beasts of the field and the birds of the heaven, He has given them into your hand, and has made you ruler over them all—you are this head of gold." (Daniel 2:37-38)

"The first was like a lion and had eagles' wings. Then as I looked its wings were plucked off, and it was lifted from the ground and made to stand on two feet like a man, and the mind of a man was given to it." (Daniel 7:4)

Jesus said in his prophecy in Luke 21:24, Jerusalem will be trampled underfoot by the Gentiles, until the times of the Gentiles are fulfilled. The times of the Gentiles are not yet fulfilled, and it will not be until this generation witness the physical presence of the future Anti-Christ causing the abomination of desolation in the Temple of the Jews in Jerusalem.

Nebuchadnezzar's Dream

Daniel 2 (NRSV)

Gold, silver, bronze, iron. The four kingdoms have been widely understood since Josephus (1st century A.D.) to be the empires of Babylon, Mede-Persia, Greece, and Rome. (The Reformation Bible)

> "In the second year of the reign of Nebuchadnezzar, Nebuchadnezzar had dreams; his spirit was troubled, and his sleep left him. Then the king commanded that the magicians, the enchanters, the sorcerers, and the Chaldeans be summoned to tell the king his dreams. So they came in and stood before the king. And the king said to them, "I had a

dream, and my spirit is troubled to know the dream."
Then the Chaldeans said to the king in Aramaic, "O
king, live forever! Tell your servants the dream, and
we will show the interpretation." (Daniel 2:1-4)

From Daniel 2:4 to 7:28, the Biblical text is in Aramaic not Hebrew. This is the only section of the Bible written in Aramaic, the language of the Babylonian Empire.

"The king answered and said to the Chaldeans, "The word from me is firm: if you do not make known to me the dream and its interpretation, you shall be torn limb from limb, and your houses shall be laid in ruins. But if you show the dream and its interpretation, you shall receive from me gifts and rewards and great honor. Therefore show me the dream and its interpretation."

They answered a second time and said, "Let the king tell his servants the dream, and we will show its interpretation." The king answered and said, "I know with certainty that you are trying to gain time, because you see that the word from me is firm–if you do not make the dream known to me, there is but one sentence for you. You have agreed to speak lying and corrupt words before me until the times change. Therefore tell me the dream, and I shall know that you can show me its interpretation." (Daniel 2:5-9)

Nebuchadnezzar formulated a test to see whether the advisers to the court access to hidden knowledge had, as they claimed. If they could not tell him the dream, then he would have no confidence in their interpretation. (The Reformation Bible)

"The Chaldeans answered the king, "There is no one on earth who can reveal what the king demands! In fact, no king, however great and powerful, has ever asked such a thing of any magician or enchanter or Chaldean. The thing that the king is asking is too difficult, and no one can reveal it to the king except the gods, whose dwelling is not with mortals."

Because of this the king flew into a violent rage and commanded that all the wise men of Babylon be destroyed.

Though he was a despot, Nebuchadnezzar knew that false religion is worse than useless. He knew that it was a curse, and he had no use for wise men that could not bring him wisdom from God.

The decree was issued, and the wise men were about to be executed; and they looked for Daniel and his companions, to execute them. Then Daniel responded with prudence and discretion to Arioch, the king's chief executioner, who had gone out to execute the wise men of Babylon; he asked Arioch, the royal official, "Why is the decree of the king so urgent?" Arioch then explained the matter to Daniel. So Daniel went in and requested that the king give him time and he would tell the king the interpretation."

https://dwellingintheword.wordpress.com/2017/12/08/2245-daniel-2/

God Reveals Nebuchadnezzar's Dream

Then Daniel went to his home and informed his companions, Hananiah, Mishael, and Azariah, and told them to seek mercy from the God of heaven concerning this mystery, so that Daniel and his companions with the rest of the wise men of Babylon might not perish.

The battle was won when Daniel prayed with his friends.

Then the mystery was revealed to Daniel in a vision of the night, and Daniel blessed the God of heaven. Daniel said:

"Blessed be the name of God from age to age,
for wisdom and power are his.
He changes times and seasons,
deposes kings and sets up kings;

he gives wisdom to the wise
and knowledge to those who have understanding.
He reveals deep and hidden things;
He knows what is in the darkness,
and light dwells with him.
To you, O God of my ancestors,
I give thanks and praise,
for you have given me wisdom and power,
and have now revealed to me what we asked of you,
or you have revealed to us what the king ordered."

Daniel Interprets the Dream

Therefore, Daniel went to Arioch, whom the king had appointed to destroy the wise men of Babylon, and said to him, "Do not destroy the wise men of Babylon; bring me in before the king, and I will give the king the interpretation."

Then Arioch quickly brought Daniel before the king and said to him: "I have found among the exiles from Judah a man who can tell the king the interpretation."

The king said to Daniel, whose name was Belteshazzar, "Are you able to tell me the dream that I have seen and its interpretation?" Daniel answered the king, "No wise men, enchanters, magicians, or diviners can show to the king the mystery that the king is asking, but there is a God in heaven who reveals mysteries, and he has disclosed to King Nebuchadnezzar what will happen at the end of days."

Just as Joseph had done in Egypt (Genesis 40:8; 41:16), so also Daniel attributes his knowledge of the dream to God. Daniel's God revealed to this young man what astrology, magic, and the occult could not discover. (The Reformation Bible)

"Your dream and the visions of your head as you lay in bed were these: To you, O king, as you lay in bed, came thoughts of what would be hereafter, and the revealer of mysteries disclosed to you what is to be. But as for me, this mystery has not been revealed to me because of any wisdom that I have more than any other living being, but in order that the interpretation may be known to the king and that you may understand the thoughts of your mind.

"You were looking, O king, and lo! there was a great statue. This statue was huge, its brilliance extraordinary; it was standing before you, and its appearance was frightening. The head of that statue was of fine gold, its chest and arms of silver, its middle and thighs of bronze, its legs of iron, its feet partly of iron and partly of clay. As you looked on, a stone was cut out, not by human hands, and it struck the statue on its feet of iron and clay and broke them in pieces. Then the iron, the clay, the bronze, the silver, and the gold, were all broken in pieces and became like the chaff of the summer threshing floors; and the wind carried them away, so that not a trace of them could be found. But the stone that struck the statue became a great mountain and filled the whole earth."

There is a progressive decrease in the value of the materials in the image from the head to the feet. Daniel first accurately reported the content of Nebuchadnezzar's dream. This gave Daniel credibility when explaining what the dream meant: the interpretation.

> "This was the dream; now we will tell the king its interpretation. You, O king, the king of kings—to whom the God of heaven has given the kingdom, the power, the might, and the glory, into whose hand he has given human beings, wherever they live, the wild animals of the field, and the birds of the air, and whom he has established as ruler over them all—you are the head of gold. After you shall arise another kingdom inferior to yours, and yet a third kingdom of bronze, which shall rule over the whole earth. And there shall be a fourth kingdom, strong as iron; just as iron crushes and smashes everything, it shall crush and shatter all these. As you saw the feet and toes partly of potter's clay and partly of iron, it shall be a divided kingdom; but some of the strength of iron shall be in it, as you saw the iron mixed with the clay. As the toes of the feet were part iron and part clay, so the kingdom shall be partly strong and partly brittle. As you saw the iron mixed with clay, so will they mix with one another in marriage, but they will not hold together, just as iron does not mix with clay. And in the days of those kings the God of heaven will set up a kingdom that shall never be destroyed."

> "Of the increase of his government and of peace there will be no end, on the throne of David and over his kingdom, to establish it and to uphold it with justice and with righteousness for this time forth and forevermore. The zeal of the lord of hosts will do this." (Isaiah 9:7)

Then the seventh angel blew his trumpet, and there were loud voices in heaven, saying, "The kingdom of the world has become the kingdom of our Lord and of his Christ, and he will reign forever and ever." (Revelation 11:15)

Daniel continues his dream interpretation. (The Reformation Bible)

> "nor shall this kingdom be left to another people. It shall crush all these kingdoms and bring them to an end, and it shall stand forever; just as you saw that a stone was cut from the mountain not by hands, and that it crushed the iron, the bronze, the clay, the silver, and the gold. The great God has informed the king what shall be hereafter. The dream is certain, and its interpretation trustworthy."

You can find all sorts of explanations for what is meant by the iron and clay portion of the image: Was it the Holy Roman Empire? Is it Europe? Which nations are represented by the ten toes of the statue? Where does the Rapture fit in? The Anti-Christ? BREXIT? Etc. Not all these answers are in this book, so I leave that research to you if you are so inclined.

Daniel and His Friends Promoted

Then King Nebuchadnezzar fell on his face, worshiped Daniel, and commanded that a grain offering, and incense be offered to him.

The king said to Daniel, "Truly, your God is God of gods and Lord of kings and a revealer of mysteries, for you have been able to reveal this mystery!" Then the king promoted Daniel, gave him many great gifts, and made him ruler over the whole province of Babylon and chief prefect over all the wise men of Babylon. Daniel made a request of the king, and he appointed Shadrach, Meshach, and Abednego over the affairs of the province of Babylon. But Daniel remained at the king's court."

The Location of Babylon

The City of Babylon was located on the eastern side of the Fertile Crescent about 55 miles of modern day south of Baghdad in Iraq. The Bible first mention of Babylon comes in Genesis 10:8 in the genealogy of Ham, "Cush was the father of Nimrod, who grew to be mighty warrior on the earth". Nimrod founded a kingdom that included a place called "Babylon" in Shinar. (Genesis 10:10) It is easy to make connection with the tower of Babel and Babylon in Genesis 11:

> "Now the whole earth had one language and the same words. And as people migrated from the east, they found a plain in the land of Shinar and settled there. And they said to one another, "Come, let us make bricks, and burn them thoroughly." And they had brick for stone, and bitumen for mortar. Then they said, "Come, let us build ourselves a city and a tower with its top in the heavens, and let us make a name for ourselves, lest we be dispersed over the face of the whole earth." And the Lord came down to see the city and the tower, which the children of man had built. And the Lord said, "Behold, they are one people, and they have all one language, and this is only the beginning of what they will do. And nothing that they propose to do will now be impossible for them. Come, let us go down and there confuses their language, so that they may not understand one another's speech." So, the Lord dispersed them from there over the face of all the earth and they left off building the city. Therefore, its name was called Babel, because there the Lord confused the language of all the earth. And from there the Lord dispersed them over the face of all the earth." (Genesis 11:1-9)

They marled the reputation of Babylonia as the city, and people rebellious to God. Babylon is mentioned from Genesis to Revelation, as it rises from its rebellious beginning to become a symbol of the Antichrist evil world system. When God's people required discipline, God used the Babylonian Empire to accomplish it, but limited Judah's captivity to 70 years.

> "And this whole land shall be desolation, and astonishment; and these nations shall serve the king of Babylon seventy years. (Jeremiah 25:11 KJV)

In today's world, it is the same place in Iraq, Mosul and Syria, Raqqa where terrorism has grown to spread across many nations. For the first time in our generation, it is in Iraq that Jihadists could behead people openly or burn them alive. ISIS has been committing all the terrible inhuman acts at their headquarters in Iraq in the city of Mosul, and Raqqa in Syria, the old Babylon city that rebelled against God. Much of the innocent Christian blood that is poured on the land of Iraq is still crying daily to God for the judgment of the people of Iraq. "They cried out with a loud voice, "O Sovereign Lord, holy and true, how long before you will judge and avenge our blood on those who dwell on the earth?" (Revelation 6:10) The judgment of God is coming soon, and Iraq and her alias are in the time line of God's prophecy.

4. Mede-Persian Empire

Also called the first Persian Empire was an Empire base western Asia. The capitals were Babylon, Susa dated 550 BC. The Mede-Persians led by King Cyrus II invaded Babylon from the east in June of 539 BC. Within a short time, Daniel became a trusted adviser to the new Mede-Persian Empire. This Kingdom of the Mede-Persian was later ruled by Artaxerxes II or Ahasuerus, who married to Esther.

Today, Persia is essentially synonymous with modern Iran, and this was not so different in ancient times. However, Persia as an ancient kingdom with Media, encompassed Egypt in the west to parts of India in the east, and included Asia Minor from the Eastern border of Greece to Tajikistan.

Prophesies

The Mede-Persian Empire foretold by Isaiah, Jeremiah, and Daniel all prophesied that the Medes and the Persians would overtake the Babylonian Empire. Isaiah quoted God as saying "see, I will stir up against them the Medes. Their bows will strike down the young men." (Daniel 13:17-18) another prophecy said that the Medes would expand be young Babylonian and affect all nations. (Jeremiah 51:28) Jeremiah also provides the reason for the Mede-Persian ascendency: "to destroy Babylon" and gain "vengeance for God's Temple" (Jeremiah 51:11).

God uses individuals and Empires to accomplish His will. Certainly, the Mede-Persia Empire is case in point. God used this Empire to set His captive free, fund the rebuilding of the Temple, and encourage His children that they are never forsaken.

The Writing on the Wall

Daniel also warned of Babylon's demise on the eve of its fall, as recorded in Daniel 5. King Belshazzar, called "king" because he was left in charge of political affairs while his father was away at war, was using the gold and silver utensils from the temple as drinking vessels in a night of debauchery. "Suddenly the fingers of a human hand appeared and wrote on the plaster of the wall" (Daniel 5:5). The frightened king summoned Daniel to the banquet hall to interpret the writing. Daniel's inspired interpretation was dire: God had pronounced judgment on Babylon, and the kingdom would be divided. By morning, "Belshazzar, king of the Babylonians, was slain, and Darius the Mede took over the kingdom" (Daniel 5:30-31).

End of the Exile

Before the Babylonian exile even began, God told Jeremiah that Judah would "become a desolate wasteland, and these nations will serve the king of Babylon seventy years" (Jeremiah 25:11). Ezra and others recorded that "in the first year of Cyrus king of Persia 539 BC, in order to fulfill the word of the Lord spoken by Jeremiah, the Lord moved the heart of Cyrus" (Ezra 1:1), and Cyrus allowed all the Jews to return to Judah. Not only did Cyrus release the Jews, but he also returned the stolen temple articles and paid for the Jews' rebuilding efforts from the royal treasury (Ezra 6:4-5). This was a monumental time in Israel's history, as Jerusalem and the temple were rebuilt, and the Law was reinstituted.

Daniel

Daniel was prominent in the Mede-Persian Empire and a trusted advisor to King Darius. However, after being placed as head of the satraps (governors of sorts), Daniel was hated by some of them for his quick ascent. They laid a legal trap for Daniel that should have gotten him killed, for he was thrown into the infamous lions' den. He survived, however, by God's intervention, and he continued to prophesy, rule, and provide counsel in that foreign land (Daniel 6:28).

Mordecai and Esther

Another key event in the history of Israel also occurred in Persia. The book of Esther describes the origin of the Feast of Purim and how the Jews were spared mass destruction. When Cyrus released the Jews to their homeland, not all of them elected to return to Judah (Esther 3:8). King Artaxerxes (or "Ahasuerus," as he is called in Esther) reigned from 404-359 BC and likely had little background on his government's history with the Jews. So, when his top advisor, Haman, accused the Jews of being routinely disobedient to the king's laws, Artaxerxes believed him and agreed to Haman's plan of genocide against the Jews. Queen Esther, herself a Jewess, had been chosen queen of the empire without disclosing her origin. In a series of remarkable events, plainly evincing God's providence, Esther was able to expose Haman's vile motives. Not only were the Jews spared destruction, but Esther's cousin Mordecai was given Haman's place of honor.

https://www.gotquestions.org/Medo-Persian-empire.html

Beauty Contest of Esther

When the king was choosing a new wife, Esther was included, and it was love at first sight for the king

http://www.freebibleimages.org/illustrations/esther-glorystory/

Esther and Mordechai

Living in the Land was a Jewish man name Mordecai, who was looking after his beautiful young cousin Esther

Esther was Jewish

But still no one knew that Esther was Jewish, not even the king

5. The Grecian Empire

The Jewish history is indelibly marked by Alexander the Great's short rule over the Grecian Empire. It was the fifth Empire to oppress Israel in the Times of Gentiles, and the third one in Daniel. It symbolizes in Daniel by the belly and thighs of Brass. "The head of the statue was made of pure gold, its chest and arms of silver, its belly and thighs of bronze as the leopard." (Daniel 2:32 NIV) "Then the third of these strange beasts appeared, and it looked like a leopard. It had four birds wing on its back, and it had four heads. Great authority was given to this beast. (Daniel 7:6) and as the he-goat (Daniel 8:5-9, 20-25)

Facts about Greece

Practically all Daniel 8 & 11 along with Revelation 6:1-8; 13:1-18; and 17:9-17; 19:19-21 must be understood in connection with the Greece which will be revived again as the eighth Kingdom. In John's day the Grecian Empire was the fifth head on the beast, which was before John in Daniel's era, and was not in John's Day. (Revelation 17:9-11).

Alexander the Great's Conquest

In 336 BC a time when Greece consisted of city states and their surrounding provinces, Alexander the Great was second to none in the speed with which he conquered new lands. In only 13 years, he defeated Syria and Egypt, brought down the Mede-Persian Empire, and went as far east as India.

Prophecy on Greece

The Grecian Kingdom was prophesied by Daniel 2 and 8 of his Book. Daniel tells of the interpretation of Nebuchadnezzar. It's dreams which foretold the Babylonia, Mede-Persian, Greek and Roman Empires.

Alexander though not named, is called "a mighty king, who will rule with power and do as he please."

> "And now I will show you the truth. Behold, three more kings shall arise in Persia, and a fourth shall be far richer than all of them. And when he has become strong through his riches, he shall stir up all against the kingdom of Greece. Then a mighty king shall arise, who shall rule with great dominion and do as he wills". (Daniel 11:2-3)

Alexander the Great carried out the plans of his father, Philip II of Macedon, to invade the Persian Empire. The war began in 336 BC when Alexander came to the throne of Greece and Macedon. He had only $75,000 (Seventy and five thousand dollars) to start the war with, while the Persian king had a yearly revenue of $11,000,000 (Eleven million dollars), many millions in the treasury, and hundreds of soldiers, besides a great navy. He had fully 50,000 Greek soldiers hired with Greek generals. But in 13 years Alexander conquered the whole Persian Empire and beyond. He literally did as he willed.

Where is Greece?

Located in the continent of Europe. Greece shares land borders with 4 countries: Macedonia, Albania, Bulgaria, Turkey.

The Hellenistic or Alexandrian Age – Daniel 11:4

This refers to the breaking up of the Grecian Empire into 4 divisions after the death of Alexander the Great. The period from Alexander to the conquest of these 4 kingdoms (336-100 BC) by the Romans is called the Hellenistic or Alexandrian Age. For a time, the generals of the army agreed to rule the various parts of the empire until Alexander's son b Roxane became of age to take the throne, but they all really desired to become king of province held. In 311 BC the child and his mother were murdered. Then the struggle for power became an open contest. Antugonus, one of the most able generals of Alexander, used Syria as a base to conquer the whole empire for himself. In 301 BC he was defeated by 4 other generals and slain. The 4 great generals then divided the empire.

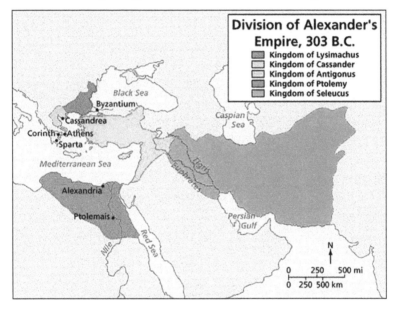

Division of Alexander's Empire, 303 B.C

Following the death of Alexander the Great in 323 BC, his successors competed for his throne. After numerous battles and shifts of allegiance, the empire was divided up among five of Alexander's generals, as shown in this map. The rivalry for power continued, however, and after the defeat of Antigonus at the Battle of Ipsus in 301 BC, there were four kingdoms. The wars lasted until 281 BC and resulted in the establishment of three main kingdoms: Egypt, Asia Minor, and Macedonia. Although the unity of the empire was gone, Greek civilization continued to spread throughout this region. The Chart above shows 5 Kingdoms instead of 4, because it still includes that of Antigonus, the first and most able general as already discussed about him.

Other 4 Generals of the Division of the Empire

1 **Cassander** took Greece, Macedon and Western parts of the empire.
2 **Lysimachus** took Asia Minor, or Present Turkey and Thrace, the northern parts of the empire.
3 **Seleucus** took all the eastern parts of the empire, including Syria and Babylon, present Iraq or the modern states of Syria, Lebanon and Iran.
4 **Ptolemy** took the kingdom of Egypt, Southern parts the empire. Thus, Alexander's empire was literally divided towards the four winds of the heaven. (Daniel 11:8)

All these division except the extreme eastern part of the kingdom of Seleucus were conquered by the Romans and made a part of the old Roman Empire out of which will be formed the 10 kingdoms of the last days. These 4 divisions of Greece will become 4 of the 10 kingdoms. They would be known today as Greece, Turkey, Syria and Egypt

6. The Holy Roman Empire

The Holy Roman Empire was a loosely joined union of smaller kingdoms which held power in western and central Europe between 962 and 1806 AD. It was ruled by a Holy Roman Emperor who oversaw local regions controlled by a variety of kings, dukes, and other officials. The Holy Roman Empire was an attempt to resurrect the Western empire of Rome.

Many people confuse the Holy Roman Empire with the Roman Empire that existed during the New Testament period. However, these two empires were different in both time and location. The

Roman Empire (27 BC–476 AD) was based in Rome (and, later, Constantinople) and controlled nations around the Mediterranean, including Israel. The Holy Roman Empire came into existence long after the Roman Empire had collapsed. It had no official capital, but the emperors usually Germanic kings ruled from their homelands.

In the fourth century, Christianity was embraced by the emperor and was pronounced the official religion of the Roman Empire. This blending of religion and government led to an uneasy but powerful mix of doctrine and politics. "Its legs were iron, and its feet were a combination of iron and baked clay" (Daniel 2:33, 40 NLT) eventually, power was consolidated in a centralized Roman Catholic Church, the major social institution throughout the middle Ages. In 1054 AD, the Eastern Orthodox Church separated from the Western (Roman) Church, in part due to Rome's centralized leadership under the Pope.

Pope Leo III laid the foundation for the Holy Roman Empire in 800 A.D when he crowned Charlemagne as emperor. This act set a precedent for the next 700 years, as the Popes claimed the right to select and install the most powerful rulers on the Continent. The Holy Roman Empire officially began in 962 A.D when Pope John XII crowned King Otto I of Germany and gave him the title of "emperor." In the Holy Roman Empire, civil authority and church authority clashed at times, but the church usually won. This was the time when the Catholic Popes wielded the most influence, and the papacy's power reached its zenith.

During the Middle Ages, a wide variety of new church traditions became official doctrine of the Roman Church. Further, the church-state engaged in many military conflicts, including the Crusades.

Late in the period of the Holy Roman Empire, a growing number of Christians grew uneasy with the dominance, teaching, and corruption of the Roman Catholic Church. In the 1500s, Martin Luther launched the Protestant Reformation. John Calvin became a Reformation leader based in Geneva, Switzerland, and others, including Ulrich Zwingli and a large Anabaptist movement, helped reform religion in the Western world.

The major theological issues in the Reformation focused on what are known as the five soles (five "onyx's"), which expressed the primacy of biblical teaching over the authority of the Pope and sacred tradition. Sola gratia, the teaching of salvation by "grace alone" through faith alone in Christ alone, empowered a new era of evangelistic outreach in Europe that extended to those who would later colonize North America. Sola scriptura, or "Scripture alone," taught that the Bible was the sole authority on matters of faith. This teaching led to the development of new churches outside of the Catholic system and the development of new statements of faith for the many Protestant groups founded during this time. The Holy Roman Empire continued to hold power after the Reformation, but the seeds of its demise had been sown; after the Reformation, the Church's imperial influence waned and the authority of the Pope was curtailed. Europe was emerging from the Middle Ages.

In summary, the Holy Roman Empire served as the government over much of Europe for most of medieval history. The Roman Catholic Church, melded in a church-state alliance with the emperor, was the major religious entity. The Church encountered numerous changes even as its amassed land and political clout. Late in this period, Martin Luther and other Reformers transformed the way religion was practiced in central Europe, and their work continues to influence many around the world today.

The Origin of the Holy Roman Empire

The Holy Roman Empire had its roots in the Roman Empire, as the Franks, a Germanic People who would eventually lend their name to France, were brought into the Northern edges of the Roman Empire as mercenaries and vassals to defend the borders from more destructive Germanic peoples further north. After the fall of the Western Roman Empire in 476 A.D, Europe descended into the so-called Dark Ages, in which literacy, communication, trade, and many forms of knowledge declined. In this period, also known as the Early Middle Ages, the kings of the Franks conquered territory roughly corresponding to France, Belgium, and Western Germany. Eventually, the famous king Charlemagne rose to the throne, and on December 25th, 800 AD, the pope crowned Charlemagne as the Holy Roman Emperor, attempting to give the impression that the ancient Roman Empire had risen again, and the union of the Church and the Empire would reclaim the previous empire.

Charlemagne's Empire in 800 (in orange)

Soon after the death of Charlemagne, though, the Holy Roman Empire lost much of its power to feuding princes, bishops, and pillaging Viking raiders, eventually becoming confined to the area roughly of modern Germany and being a weak, decentralized, ineffective government until its conquest and dissolution by Napoleon in the early 1800s.

To quote the famous line, "The Holy Roman Empire was neither Holy, nor Roman, nor an Empire" – Voltaire

7. The Roman Empire

The Roman Empire was centered on Rome, Italy, and is considered to have lasted from 27 BC until 476 AD. It was formed from the Roman Republic before it, with roots stretching back from the 8th century BC. The Eastern Portion of the Roman Empire, also known as the Byzantine Empire, survived the fall of the Western Empire until 1453 AD.

Roman People

Jesus' Prophecy Fulfilled in 70 AD by General Titus of Rome

> "Jesus left the temple and was going away when his disciples came to point out to him the buildings of the temple. But he answered them, "You see all these, do you not? Truly, I say to you, there will not be left here one stone upon another that will not be thrown down" (Matthew 24:12 c.f. Daniel 9:26-27 & Luke 21:20-24)

Rome oppressed Israel over 200 years and dispersed the Jews led by General Titus of Rome.

Gessius Florus loved money and hated Jews. As Roman procurator, he ruled Judea, caring little for their religious sensibilities. When tax revenues were low, he seized silver from the temple. As the uproar against him grew, in 66 AD, he sent troops into Jerusalem who massacred 3,600 citizens. Florus's action touched off an explosive rebellion the First Jewish Revolt that had been sizzling for some time.

Timeline of the year 66 AD

According to Josephus, the violence of the year 66 AD initially began at Caesarea, provoked by Greeks of a certain merchant house sacrificing birds in front of a local synagogue. The Roman garrison did not intervene there and thus the long-standing Hellenistic and Jewish religious tensions took a downward spiral. In reaction, one of the Jewish Temple clerks Eleazar ben Hanania ceased prayers and sacrifices for the Roman emperor at the Temple.

Protests over taxation joined the list of grievances and random attacks on Roman citizens and perceived 'traitors' occurred in Jerusalem. Tension reached a breaking point when Roman governor Gessius Florus sent Roman troops to remove seventeen talents from the Temple treasury, claiming the money was for unpaid taxes.

In response to this action, the city of Jerusalem fell into unrest and some of the Jewish population began to openly mock Florus by passing a basket around to collect money as if Florus was poor. Rioters even attacked a garrison, killing the soldiers. Even the ensuing intervention of the Syrian governor, who discovered he could not help. Florus reacted to the unrest by sending soldiers into Jerusalem the next day to raid the city and arrest several city leaders, who were later whipped and crucified, despite many of them being Roman citizens.

Aftermath

Shortly, outraged Judean nationalist factions took up arms and the Roman military garrison of Jerusalem was quickly overrun by rebels. In September 66, the Romans in Jerusalem surrendered and were lynched. Meanwhile, the Greek inhabitants of the capital of Judaea, Caesarea, attacked their Jewish neighbors; the Jews replied in kind, expelling many Greeks from Judaea, Galilee and the Golan heights. Fearing the worst, the pro-Roman king Agrippa II and his sister Berenice fled Jerusalem to Galilee. Judean militias later moved upon Roman citizens of Judaea and pro-Roman officials, cleansing the country of any Roman symbols.

https://en.wikipedia.org/wiki/Jerusalem_riots_of_66

Launching the Revolt

The Jewish Revolt began and met its bitter end at Masada, a hunk of rock overlooking the Dead Sea. The Romans had built a virtually impregnable fortress there. Yet the atrocities of Florus inspired some crazy Zealots to attack Masada. Amazingly, they won, slaughtering the Roman army there.

In Jerusalem, the temple captain signified solidarity with the revolt by stopping the daily sacrifices to Caesar. Soon all Jerusalem was in an uproar, expelling or killing the Roman troops. Then all Judea was in revolt; then Galilee.

Cestius Callus, the Roman governor of the region, marched from Syria with twenty thousand soldiers. He besieged Jerusalem for six months yet failed. He left six thousand dead Roman soldiers, not to mention weaponry that the Jewish defenders picked up and used.

Emperor Nero then sent Vespasian, a decorated general, to quell the Judean rebellion. Vespasian put down the opposition in Galilee, then in Transjordan, then in Idumean. He circled in on Jerusalem.

But before the coup de grace, Nero died. Vespasian became embroiled in a leadership struggle that concluded with the eastern armies calling for him to be emperor. One of his first imperial acts was to appoint his son Titus to conduct the Jewish War.

Crushing the Revolt

By now, Jerusalem was isolated from the rest of the nation, and factions within the city fought over strategies of defense. As the siege wore on, people began dying from starvation and plague. The high priest's wife, who once basked in luxury, scavenged for crumbs in the streets.

Meanwhile the Romans employed new war machines to hurl boulders against the city walls. Battering rams assaulted the fortifications. Jewish defenders fought all day and struggled to rebuild the walls at night. Eventually the Romans broke through the outer wall, then the second wall, and finally the third wall. Still the Jews fought, scurrying to the temple as their last line of defense.

That was the end for the valiant Jewish defenders and for the temple. Historian Josephus claimed that Titus wanted to preserve the temple, but his soldiers were so angry at their resilient opponents that they burned it. The remaining Jews were slaughtered or sold as slaves. The Zealot band that took Masada held it for at least three more years. When the Romans finally built their siege ramp and invaded the mountain fortress, they found the defenders dead they had committed suicide to avoid being captured by foreigners.

Results of the Revolt

The Jewish Revolt marked the end of the Jewish state until the modern state of Israel was formed in 1948 (see page 217-8). The destruction of the temple also signified a change in the Jews' worship (although that change had begun as Jews had been scattering throughout the world for at least six hundred years). The first destruction of the temple, by the Babylonians in 586 BC, had forced the Jews to become people of the Book. The temple's sad end slammed the door on the Jew's sacrificial system. They adjusted, of course, creating new rituals for home and synagogue. But the Sanhedrin was dissolved, and the center of Jewish religion moved to the educational institutions of Jamnia.

8. The Revised Roman Empire

The Revised Roman Empire is the next Empire mentioned in scripture as oppressing Israel in the Times of the Gentiles. This Kingdom will be made up of 10 Kingdoms inside the Roman Empire Territory in the last days. For this reason, it is called the Revised and not the Revived.

Now if the Roman Empire will be revived, then we are to expect only one Kingdom rule by one man inside the old Roman Empire, but instead ten separate Kingdoms ruled by ten Kings and with ten separate capitals will be formed inside the Roman Empire territory. This is symbolized in Daniel by the ten toes:

> "And there shall be a fourth kingdom, strong as iron, because iron breaks to pieces and shatters all things. And like iron that crushes, it shall break and crush all these. And as you saw the feet and toes, partly of potter's clay and partly of iron, it shall be a divided kingdom, but some of the firmness of iron shall be in it, just as you saw iron mixed with the soft clay. And as the toes of the feet were partly iron and partly clay, so the kingdom shall be partly strong and partly brittle. As you saw the iron mixed with soft clay, so they will mix with one another in marriage, but they will not hold together, just as iron does not mix with clay. And in the days of those kings the God of heaven will set up a kingdom that

shall never be destroyed, nor shall the kingdom be left to another people. It shall break in pieces all these kingdoms and bring them to an end, and it shall stand forever, just as you saw that a stone was cut from a mountain by no human hand, and that it broke in pieces the iron, the bronze, the clay, the silver, and the gold. A great God has made known to the king what shall be after this. The dream is certain, and its interpretation sure" (Daniel 2:40-45)

Horns are the other symbol, which in the context of Daniel are representative of kings or political powers: "After this I saw in the night visions, and behold, a fourth beast, terrifying and dreadful and exceedingly strong. It had great iron teeth; it devoured and broke in pieces and stamped what was left with its feet. It was different from all the beasts that were before it, and it had ten horns. I considered the horns, and behold, there came up among them another horn, a little one, before which three of the first horns were plucked up by the roots. And behold, in this horn were eyes like the eyes of a man, and a mouth speaking great things" (Daniel 7:7-8, 9-24). This is echoed by the ten horns in Revelation. (Revelation 12:3; 13:1; 17:9-17).

Understanding the Revised Roman Empire as distinct from the Revived Grecian Empire

1. The seven heads are: Egypt, Assyria, Babylon, Mede-Persia, Greece, Rome, and Revised Rome that is yet to come. The 10 horns are the 10-nation confederacy that will make up the revised Roman Empire (Daniel 7:8, 7: 23-24; Revelation 17:12). The 10 crowns are its 10 kings; they are also the 10 toes of Daniel 2:41-44.

2. The Roman Empire was not "wounded unto death," or conquered from without. Its demise was from within. It has, however, never ceased to exist even unto this day. The Grecian Empire, on the other hand, did receive a mortal wound from Rome, although its 4 divisions Greece, Turkey, Syria, and Egypt continue until

today. It is Greece, then, that will be resurrected or revived as the eighth kingdom to oppress the nation Israel (Revelation 17:10-11). Today, the Roman Empire is beginning to be revised not revived in the European Economic Community (Revelation 17:12). In the years to come, however, for the prophecies of the 10 horns and 10 toes of Daniel to manifest, the 10-nation confederacy that will comprise the revised Roman Empire must include the above 4 divisions of the Grecian Empire. Daniel makes this very clear at Daniel 8:9, 8:21-23, and 11:40. These 10 nations will be in the territories formally ruled by both Rome and Greece, as the Bible clearly states that the 10-horn nations of revived Greece must come out of revised Rome (Daniel 7:24; Revelation 17:11).

We must also remember that there were 5 toes on each of the feet of iron and clay on the image God gave to King Nebuchadnezzar (Daniel 2:41-44). The legs, feet and toes represent the Roman and revised Roman empires. At the close of the 3rd century AD, the Roman emperor, Diocletian, divided the Roman Empire into two main divisions east and west. In 395 AD the emperor Theodosius I made this division official by dividing the empire between his two sons. Rome became the capital of the Western Roman Empire and Constantinople [Byzantium] became the capital of the Eastern Roman Empire. [To precisely fulfill Bible prophecy, then, we should look for a confederacy of nations with 5 of the toe/nations to be on each foot of revised Roman Empire five from the West and five from the East.]

The revised Roman Empire does not actually come into existence until it is given a king ruling over the entire confederacy. He will continue but a short space (Revelation 17:10). By the middle of The Antichrist Covenant week, the kings of these 10 nations will come to hate the great whore city of Mystery Babylon and will agree to destroy her [see The Mystery of Mystery Babylon]. They will burn her with fire. They will then give their power, authority and kingdom to the Antichrist (Revelation 17:13, 16-17), whose kingdom then becomes the revived Grecian Empire.

3. The same time of Gentile rule of Jerusalem (Revelation 11:2) and the ministry of the two witnesses (Revelation 11:3): the last half of both the Antichrist Covenant Week and Daniel's 70th week.

4. People are missing, because the remnant of Israel is hidden in the wilderness (Revelation 12:6 &14).

5. It is my opinion that the false prophet will be the Jewish high priest and not the Pope. This fits the detailed historical pattern established in 1st and 2nd Maccabees in the collusion between the Jason, the Jewish high priest, and in Antiochus Epiphanes, the biblical model of the Antichrist (Daniel 11:21-34). As a matter of fact, the Pope is excluded on geographical grounds because since the Greek Empire never ruled Italy and Rome. Likewise, the revived Grecian Empire will not include the nation of Italy, and thus excludes the Vatican City.

6. There is a strong suggestion given the amount of repetition concerning the deadly wound that was healed (Revelation 13:3, 12, 14) that the Antichrist [the counterfeit savior] may also personally receive and recover from a deadly wound.

7. It is the false prophet that demands worship of the Antichrist. He is also the one who institutes to mark of the beast computer system.

8. When one "counts" the number 666 he gets the number up to 18. A person living in the United States of America could very well have as his number 666, followed by a 3-digit country code (011), followed by a 3-digit area code (301), and then a 9-digit social security number (647-58-7868) making a total of 18 digits. With a laser gun, such a number could be instantly, painlessly and invisibly inserted on the hand or forehead of any person and used to control buying and selling with the present scanners in today's supermarkets.

[See When Your Money Fails 666 and The New Money System, by Mary Stewart Relfe, Ph.D., Ministries, Inc., P. O. Box 4038, Montgomery, Al 36104.

9. This is following the end of The Antichrist Covenant Week and Daniel's 70th week and the war in the heavenly realm (Revelation 12:7).

10. The chronological story continues from the war in the heavenly realm and third woe of Satan and his angels being cast into the earth (Revelation 12:7-12). Angels must preach the gospel because both the two witnesses and the 144,000 have been taken to heaven (Revelation 11:12 & 14:1).

11. Literal Babylon (Revelation 18).

12. These are not angels, but redeemed men [Revelation 17:1, 19:8, 19:10, 19:14, 21:9, 22:1, 22:6-9].

DETAILS

Therefore, it is not one horn on the beast, symbolizing one king reigning from Rome over one king, as was true of the old Roman Empire, but ten kings out this Kingdom. Again, this means that there will be a Revised Roman Empire, not a Revived Roman Empire.

This further means that, there must another great European, Asiatic, and African war to form ten future kingdoms out of the 24 present states of the old Roman Empire territory:

> "And in the latter time of their kingdom, When the transgressors have reached their fullness, A king shall arise, having fierce features, who understands sinister schemes. His power shall be mighty, but not by his own power; He shall destroy fearfully and

shall prosper and thrive; He shall destroy the mighty, and the holy people." (Daniel 8:23-24 NKJV)

That these ten kingdoms are yet future and will exist and reign together inside the old Roman Empire territory is clear from the study of the 8 Mountain Kingdoms. They will not include the entire world, only the then Roman Empire, and part of Southern Europe, Western Asia, and Northern Africa.

9. The Revived Grecian Empire

The Antichrist: The Revived Grecian Empire

"And I saw a beast rising out of the sea, [this beast is the Antichrist (Daniel 7:3), with ten horns and seven heads, with ten diadems on its horns and blasphemous names on its heads. And the beast that I saw was like a leopard [Greece]; its feet were like a bear's, [Mede-Persia] and its mouth was like a lion's mouth [Babylon]. And to it the dragon [the Antichrist's power comes from Satan] gave his power and his throne and great authority. One of its heads seemed to have a mortal wound, [Greece] but its mortal wound was healed, and the whole earth marveled as they followed the beast. And they worshiped the dragon, for he had given his authority to the beast, and they worshiped the beast, saying, "Who is like the beast, and who can fight against it?" And the beast was given a mouth uttering haughty and blasphemous words, and it was allowed to exercise authority for forty-two months. 6It opened its mouth to utter blasphemies against God, blaspheming his name and his dwelling, that is, those who dwell in heaven. Also it was allowed to make war on the saints and to conquer them. [Daniel 7:21

& 7:25] And authority was given it over every tribe and people and language and nation, and all who dwell on earth will worship it, everyone whose name has not been written before the foundation of the world in the book of life of the Lamb who was slain. If anyone has an ear, let him hear. If anyone is to be taken captive, to captivity he goes; if anyone is to be slain with the sword, with the sword must he be slain. Here is a call for the endurance and faith of the saints." (Revelation 13:1-10) [The saints will not be able to resist the Antichrist with physical force–Revelation 14:12-13].

This identifies the time of fulfillment of the main purpose of the vision in the book of Daniel. (Daniel 11:40; 8:19; 9:27; 11:35, 11:45; 12:1, 12:7-13) and will be the second of the future Empire to oppress Israel in the times of the Gentiles, and the last world power to do so.

The vision concerns the very end of the Gentile world powers symbolized by the image of Daniel 2 and the beast of Daniel 7 and 8, Revelation 13; 17:8-17. At the time of the end of this age in which we live, shall the king of the south (Egypt) put him (that is the king of the North Syria) to come against him (that is, the king of the south, Egypt) like a whirlwind with his armies and navies and conquer many countries. (Daniel 11:40)

The above quotations refer to the little horn or the Antichrist coming out of the ten horns of the Revised Rome; And after them to get power over in the 3 1/2 years of Daniel's 70th week. The Antichrist will overthrow 3 of the divisions (Greece, Turkey, and Egypt) the other 6 will submit to him, thus making him their leader forming the 8th Kingdom in a war with the north and east. (Daniel 7:6, 23-24; Revelation 13:1-2; 17:8-17) to revive the old Grecian Empire, which is symbolized by a leopard.

He comes from Syria, one of the 4 divisions of the Grecian Empire. "Out of one of them came a little horn, which grew exceedingly great toward the south, toward the east, and toward the glorious land. (Daniel 8:9) "And at the latter end of their kingdom, when the transgressors have reached their limit, a king of bold face, one who understands riddles, shall arise". (Daniel 8:23)

"And the king shall do as he wills. He shall exalt himself and magnify himself above every god and shall speak astonishing things against the God of gods. He shall prosper till the indignation is accomplished; for what is decreed shall be done. He shall pay no attention to the gods of his fathers, or to the one beloved by women. He shall not pay attention to any other god, for he shall magnify himself above all. He shall honor the god of fortresses instead of these. A god whom his fathers did not know he shall honor with gold and silver, with precious stones and costly gifts. He shall deal with the strongest fortresses with the help of a foreign god. Those who acknowledge him he shall load with honor. He shall make them rulers over many and shall divide the land for a price. "At the time of the end, the king of the south shall attack him, but the king of the north shall rush upon him like a whirlwind, with chariots and horsemen, and with many ships. And he shall come into countries and shall overflow and pass through. He shall come into the glorious land. And tens of thousands shall fall, but these shall be delivered out of his hand: Edom and Moab and the main part of the Ammonites. He shall stretch out his hand against the countries, and the land of Egypt shall not escape. He shall become ruler of the treasures of gold and of silver, and all the precious things of Egypt, and the Libyans and the Cushites shall follow in his train. But news from the east and the north shall alarm him, and he shall go out with great fury to destroy and devote many to destruction. And he shall pitch his palatial tents between the sea and the glorious holy mountain. Yet he shall come to his end, with none to help him." (Daniel 11:36-45).

5

The 70th Week of Daniel's Prophecy

Daniel had read the prophecies of Jeremiah and understood that Israel would be in Babylonian captivity for a period of seventy (70) years. He knew that the 70-year period was almost complete, but they have not seen any sign of redemption coming:

> "For thus says the Lord: When seventy years are completed for Babylon, I will visit you, and I will fulfill to you my promise and bring you back to this place. For I know the plans I have for you, declares the Lord, plans for welfare and not for evil, to give you a future and a hope. Then you will call upon me and come and pray to me, and I will hear you. You will seek me and find me when you seek me with all your heart. I will be found by you, declares the Lord, and I will restore your fortunes and gather you from all the nations and all the places where I have driven you, declares the Lord, and I will bring you back to the place from which I sent you into exile". (Jeremiah 29:10-14)

Daniel, was seeking the LORD in prayer and fasting for what his people were to do, when the time of their captivity is completed.

Gabriel brings an answer

"While I was speaking and praying, confessing my
sin and the sin of my people Israel, and presenting
my plea before the Lord my God for the holy hill
of my God, while I was speaking in prayer, the man
Gabriel, whom I had seen in the vision at the first,
came to me in swift flight at the time of the evening sacrifice. He made me understand, speaking
with me and saying, "O Daniel, I have now come
out to give your insight and understanding. At the
beginning of your pleas for mercy a word went out,
and I have come to tell it to you, for you are greatly
loved. Therefore, consider the word and understand
the vision." (Daniel 9:20-23)

The Seventy Weeks

"Seventy weeks are decreed about your people and
your holy city, to finish the transgression, to put
an end to sin, and to atone for iniquity, to bring in
everlasting righteousness, to seal both vision and
prophecy, and to anoint a most holy place. Know
therefore and understand that from the going out
of the word to restore and build Jerusalem to the
coming of an anointed one, a prince, there shall be
seven weeks. Then for sixty-two weeks it shall be
built again with squares and moat, but in a troubled
time. And after the sixty-two weeks, an anointed
one shall be cut off and shall have nothing. And the
people of the prince who is to come shall destroy
the city and the sanctuary. Its end shall come with a
flood, and to the end there shall be war. Desolations
are decreed. And he shall make a strong covenant
with many for one week, and for half of the week
he shall put an end to sacrifice and offering. And
on the wing of abominations shall come one who

makes desolate, until the decreed end is poured out on the desolator." (Daniel 9:24-27)

Meaning

In the NIV Bible, verse 24 reads "Seventy 'sevens' (70x7) are decreed for your people and your holy city to finish transgression, to put an end to sin, to atone for wickedness, to bring in ever-lasting righteousness, to seal up vision and prophecy and to anoint the Most Holy Place. In Hebrew week is shavua and is translated seven. Therefore, seventy weeks are (seventy times seven = 490) was interpreted to Daniel as 70x7 = 490 years of period has been decreed for the Jews to be in exile, to fulfil their punishment by God. This week of seven prophecy goes beyond to the tribulation that Jesus prophesied in Matthew: "For then shall be great tribulation, such as was not since the beginning of the world to this time, no, nor ever shall be". (Matthew 24:21 KJV) Jesus was prophesying about Daniel's 70th week.

Divisions of the Seventy Weeks

According to the angel Gabriel's interpretation to Daniel, each week represents one seven (1 week = 7). We see how the NIV and then the KJV renders verse 25:

> "Know and understand this: From the time the word goes out to restore and rebuild Jerusalem until the Anointed One, the ruler, comes, there will be seven 'sevens,' [7x7 = 49 + 62x7 = 483] and sixty-two 'sevens.' It will be rebuilt with streets and a trench, but in times of trouble." (Daniel 9:25 NIV)

> "Know therefore and understand, that from the going forth of the commandment to restore and to build Jerusalem unto the Messiah the Prince shall be seven weeks, and threescore and two weeks: the

street shall be built again, and the wall, even in troublous times." (Daniel 9:25 KJV)

Threescore means 20x3 = 60 and 2 weeks (60+2=62 weeks). One
score represent 20. To better understand this calculation, let me
put it in a form of writing a bank cheque of 62 dollars. (Sixty and
two dollars only), from the going forth of the commandment to
restore and build Jerusalem until Messiah the Prince. You may
write "Sixty and two".

Verse 27 says; "And he shall confirm the covenant with many
for one week [= 7 years]; and during the week he shall cause the
sacrifice and the oblation to cease, and for the overspreading of
abominations he shall make it desolate, even until the consum-
mation, and that determined shall be poured upon the desolate."
(Daniel 9:27 KJV)

So now 62 weeks plus one week of seven, (62+7=69 weeks. If
now the total weeks comes to 69, and one week stands for seven
(7), then we could multiply 69x7 = 483 years in exile. Remember
Daniel was looking to literal 70 years, if so, then let me subtract 69
from 70 (70-69 =1), thus the Angel said 70x7, seventy sevens in
NIV will give us 490 and the understanding of this interpretation
"seven" stand for week(s), However, it's now remained one week
(1 week) when subtract 69 weeks from 70 weeks.

On the other hand, the total years of seventy weeks (70 weeks
comes to 70x7 = 490 less 62x7 weeks + 7x7 weeks = 483 years.
(490-483=7). 7 years = 1 weeks now remains to fulfill the entire
prophecy of the Bible decreed about the Jews.

The above calculation of prophecy indicates that, God suspended
His contract with the Jewish punishment when it was left with
7 years (one week). So, this is what the Bible calls "The time
of Jacobs trouble, (Jeremiah 30:7), and as Jesus call it the Great
Tribulation in Matthew 24:21

Note that this prophecy is determined for Daniel's people (the Jews) and for his Holy city (Jerusalem). It is however important to know that this is not determined upon the church. The Church will be Raptured before the Great Tribulation or during and beginning of the first 3 and half years. Also, it is the time to fulfill the phrase in Luke chapter 21:24, "Until the time of the Gentiles be fulfilled" during the war of Armageddon.

First Period

The first period consisted of seven sevens (7x7) of years, or 49 years during which the Holy City, its streets, and walls were to be build "even in troublous times (Daniel 9:25), began in the month of Nisan April in the 20th year of king Artaxerxes in 445 BC. "Thus, 490 years began with the commandment to restore Jerusalem unto the Messiah".

There were three decrees of the reign of Cyrus, king of Persia (Ezra 1:1-4; 3:8; Isaiah 44:28; 45:1-4; 46:11).

Cyrus reigned nine years, then Cambyses, his son reigned seven years. In the reign of Cambyses, the work on the temple and city ceased Ezra 4:1-24. Darius I of profane history reigned thirty-five years. In the second year of his reign he reconfirmed the decree made by Cyrus and the work was started again. The Temple was finished in the sixth year of his reign, but was not then restored although fifty-seven years had passed since the first decree was made by Cyrus Ezra 6:1-15.

Xerxes ruled from 486 BC until his assassination in 465 BC at the hands of Artabanus, the commander of the royal bodyguard. Xerxes 1 is one of the Persian kings, associated by modern commentators with, and identified as Ahasuerus in the Biblical book of Esther, also mentioned as a king of Persia in Ezra. He is also notable in Western history for his failed invasion of Greece in 480 BC. He is part of Daniel's description in chapter 11:14. Artaxerxes reigned after Xerxes twenty years and he then gave the third decree to Nehemiah to restore "Jerusalem unto the Messiah" (Nehemiah 2:1-6:19; Daniel 9:25, 26). Nehemiah restored the walls in fifty-two days after he reached Jerusalem, but this was by no means the full restoration. That took place seven sevens or forty-nine years after the third decree, which was given about 452 BC.

> "In the month of Nisan, in the twentieth year of King Artaxerxes, when wine was before him, I took up the wine and gave it to the king. Now I had not been sad in his presence. And the king said to me, "Why is your face sad, seeing you are not sick? This is nothing but sadness of the heart." Then I was very much afraid. I said to the king, "Let the king live forever! Why should not my face be sad, when the city, the place of my fathers' graves, lies in ruins, and its gates have been destroyed by fire?" Then the king said to me, "What are you requesting?" So, I prayed to the God of heaven. And I said to the king, "If it pleases the king, and if your servant has found favor in your sight, that you send me to Judah, to the city of my fathers' graves, that I may rebuild it." And the king said to me (the queen sitting beside him), "How long will you be gone, and when will you return?" So, it pleased the king to send me when I had given him a time. And I said to the king, "If it pleases the king, let letters be given me to the governors of the province Beyond the River, that they may let me pass through until I come to Judah, and a letter to Asaph, the keeper of the king's forest, that he may give me timber to make beams for the gates of the fortress of the temple, and for the wall of the city, and for the house that I shall occupy." And the king granted me what I asked, for the good hand of my God was upon me. (Nehemiah 2:1-8)

Another Biblical reference to a week equaling 7 years can be found in Genesis chapter 29:

> "Fulfil her week, and we will give thee this also for the service which thou shalt serve with me yet seven other years. And Jacob did so and fulfilled her week: and he gave him Rachel his daughter to wife also." (Genesis 29:27-28 KJV)

Second Period

The second period consists of sixty-two sevens (62x7 = 434) years or was threescore and two weeks 60+2. One score stand for 20, therefore threescore will be sixty and two weeks making the total sixty-two weeks (60 and 2 = 62 weeks). Now if one week is seven, then we have 62x7 = 434 years + the first period of 7x7 =49 will give a total of 483 years on time. It began immediately after the first period of seven sevens or forty-nine and continued without a break to the time when the Messiah will be cut off means Jesus will be crucified around that time of 483 years remaining 7 years. (Daniel 9:26).

This phrase "cut off" is the Hebrew karath, meaning "to cut off in death" (Genesis 9:11; Deuteronomy 20:20; Jeremiah 11:19; Psalms 37:9). These forty-nine and 434 years make 483 years from the third decree to the crucifixion of the Messiah, or sixty-nine of the seventy sevens of years, leaving the last period of seven years concerning Israel and Jerusalem to fulfil after the crucifixion.

Salvation Extended to Gentiles

For in the month of Nisan April AD 32 Jesus Christ of Nazareth was crucified "He came to his own [some 30 years ago], and his own people did not receive him. But to all who did receive him, who believed in his name, he gave the right to become children of

God." (John 1:11-12) "For by grace you have been saved through faith. And this is not your own doing; it is the gift of God, not a result of works, so that no one may boast." (Ephesians 2:8-9)

Notes:

a). For this calculation, we use the Hebrew prophetic years of 360 days = 1 year. These 360 days years go all the way back to the flood in calculating Hebrew years. "For in seven days I will send rain on the earth forty days and forty nights, and every living thing that I have made I will blot out from the face of the ground." "And in the seventh month, on the seventeenth day of the month, the ark came to rest on the mountains of Ararat. (Genesis 7:4; 8:4)

By using 360-day years, the time from Nehemiah's commission by king Artaxerxes to build the wall and city until Christ was crucified comes out to be exactly 483 years.

b). The prophecy declares that Daniel should "know and understand" that from the going forth of the command to restore and rebuild Jerusalem, until the Messiah the Prince comes, that there will be sixty and two seven sevens of years. Therefore, if a seven (shabua) is seven years, then 69 sevens is 483 years (69 x 7 = 483 years). Some scholars believe that at that time in history most of the known accent calendars calculated a year as 360 days (Hebrew, Mayan, Egyptian, Babylonian and many others). Some scholars believe an astronomical event (e.g., a close passing of Mars, a meteor or comet striking the earth) lengthened the time the earth takes to rotate time around the sun to the current 365.25 days per year. Scholars also believe that for prophetic calendars the Jews used a 360-day calendar year. The 360 days per calendar year by the 483 years to get the 173,880 days. Gabriel was telling Daniel that 173,880 days after the command is given to "restore and rebuild Jerusalem" the Messiah would come. Remember, as the time this prophecy was given, the city of Jerusalem was desolated.

https://www.iclnet.org/pub/resources/text/m.sion/jewc70da.htm

Third Period

Thus the third period of seventy sevens (70 x7= 490) of years was limited to 483 years, which God determined for the city and the people of Israel. This better known as Daniel's seventieth week. The crucifixion of the Messiah ended the sixty-ninth week and God ceased dealing with Israel as a nation to date. They were broken off in unbelief and their city destroyed as foretold in this same vision of seventy weeks Daniel 9:26; and by Jesus in Matthew 21:43; 23:37-39; 24:2; Luke 21:20-24. Also, we see Acts 13:45-49; Romans 11. This seventieth week will be fulfilled when Israel, partially gathered, will exist as a nation in possession of Jerusalem. That Jerusalem will be in their possession again is proved by the fact that it will again be given to Gentiles in the middle of the week (Revelation 11:1-2)

We see recently, in 2018, American President Donald J, Trump signed into effect that Jerusalem should remained the capital of Israel. We also understand that since no one can reverse that signing, that Jerusalem will thus remain capital until Daniel's seventieth week is fulfilled. Apart from Jerusalem being restored back to the Jews as their Capital, the rest of the prophecies are yet to be fulfilled. The 70th Week will be the last seven years dispensation and will parallel the seven years covenant between Antichrist and Israel (Daniel 9:27). It is to be the time when all the events Revelation 6:1-19:2 will be fulfilled, and when the whole tribulation will run its course. What is to happen during this week was not revealed to Daniel in detail, but it was revealed to John. This week of years will begin after the rapture of the Church, and at the second advent, and complete all the remaining prophesied events of the Bible concerning Israel. The present Church Age comes in between the sixty-ninth week and seventieth weeks, or during the time of Israel's rejection.

The 7 years which Israel has not yet fulfilled till Jesus was born to save mankind is very important in the echelon of Bible history and prophecy.

The seven-year period which make to 490 of total years of Israel's suffering is still in God's timetable and is decreed to fulfill in this generation anytime soon.

The period is divided onto two parts 3 and ½ years 3 ½ years or 1,062 days, in which the Antichrist will rule the world as the world's president or last world leader.

"God's plan for man". Expanded index edition – by Finis Jennings Dake–Page 792

The Gap

The aspect which God did not reveal to Daniel was that, there was to be a long gap or period between the first coming of Christ and the fulfillment of the 70th week his second coming. "This message was kept secret for centuries and generations past, but now it has been revealed to God's people. "Which was not made known to people in other generations as it has now been revealed by the Spirit to God's holy apostles and prophets" (Ephesians 5:3; Colossians 1:26 NIV).

This Gap comes between verses 26-27 of Daniel 9. In Isaiah 61:1-2, the Prophet said that there would be a gap between the first coming and the second coming. "The Spirit of the Lord God is upon me, because the Lord has anointed me to bring good news to the poor; he has sent me to bind up the brokenhearted, to proclaim liberty to the captives, and the opening of the prison to those who are bound; to proclaim the year of the Lord's favor, and the day of vengeance of our God; to comfort all who mourn." (Isaiah 61:1-2). This interval is confirmed by Luke in his account of Jesus reading in the synagogue, where Jesus stops halfway through verse 2 omitting "the day of vengeance of our God", and only confirming verse 1 and the first part of verse 2 as fulfilled by Him at His first coming. (Luke 4:18-19)

6

The Identity of the Antichrist

M any people have a different picture and perception of who will be the world future leader, and particularly where the future Antichrist will come from. Some even argue that the Antichrist is already here. Others are quick to point the finger at the current Pope of the Roman Catholic Church. There was a time people were even saying the Antichrist will be Barack Obama of the United States of America. Then President Trump came, and they started pointing fingers at him as the Antichrist too. Fingers have been pointed to previous Popes and none of them happened to be the Antichrist. Although Rome and the Papacy will play a significant role in the last days.

The Antichrist is male and human, but as at the time of writing this book, he is unknown, and he is not any man now prominent in today's world affairs.

> "Also, it causes all, both small and great, both rich and poor, both free and slave, to be marked on the right hand or the forehead, so that no one can buy or sell unless he has the mark, that is, the name of the beast or the number of its name. This calls for wisdom: let the one who has understanding calcu-late the number of the beast, for it is the number of a man, and his number is 666" (Revelation 13:16-17)

When one "counts" the number 666 he gets the number up to 18. A person living in the United States of America could very well have as his number as 666, followed by a 3-digit country code (011), followed by a 3-digit area code (240), and then a 9-digit social security number (110-44-8628) making a total of 18 digits. With a laser gun, such a number could be instantly, painlessly and invisibly inserted on the hand or forehead of any person and used to control buying and selling with the present scanners in today's supermarkets.

[See When Your Money Fails 666 and The New Money System, by Mary Stewart Relfe, Ph.D., Ministries, Inc., P. O. Box 4038, Montgomery, Al 36104.]

Micro-Chip Implants

All this technology is leading up to the mark of the beast system. 666

The 666 Barcode

https://heiscomingblog.wordpress.com/2015/02/13/what-if-you-were-legally-required-to-get-chipped-as-a-condition-of-employment-the-laws-are-being-discussed-now/

> "Let no one deceive you in any way. For that day will not come, unless the rebellion comes first, and the man of lawlessness is revealed, the son of destruction" (2 Thessalonians 2:3).

The Antichrist will not come on the scene of action until after the 10 kingdoms are formed inside the old Roman Empire territory.

> "Thus, he said: 'As for the fourth beast, there shall be a fourth kingdom on earth, which shall be different from all the kingdoms, and it shall devour the whole earth, and trample it down, and break it to pieces. As for the ten horns, out of this kingdom ten kings shall arise, and another shall arise after them; he shall be different from the former ones and shall put down three kings. (Daniel 7:23-24).

"And until after the rapture of the Church, "For the mystery of lawlessness is already at work. Only he who now restrains it will do so until he is out of the way. And then the lawless one will be revealed, whom the Lord Jesus will kill with the breath of his mouth and bring to nothing by the appearance of his coming." (2 Thessalonians 2:7-8)

He will come at the beginning of Daniel's 70th week (Daniel 9:27; Revelation 6:1-2) and from Syria, as the little horn. (Daniel 8:9, 20-25; 7:23-24; 11:36-45) The Antichrist is the king of the north (Syria) Aram.

"The sons of Shem: Elam, Asshur, Arpachshad, Lud, and Aram. (Genesis 10:22) Who fights the king of the south Egypt:

"For the king of the north shall again raise a multitude, greater than the first; And after some years he shall come on with a great army and abundant supplies. In those times many shall rise against the king of the south (Egypt), and the violent among your own people shall lift themselves up to fulfill the vision, but they shall fail. Then the king of the north (Syria) shall come and throw up siege works and take a well-fortified city. And the forces of the south (Egypt) shall not stand, or even his best troops, for there shall be no strength to stand. But he who comes against him shall do as he wills, and none shall stand before him. And he shall stand in the glorious land, with destruction in his hand." (Daniel 11:13-16)

He is identified as Assyrian (Asshur). (Genesis 10:22; Isaiah 10:24; 14:25; 30:31; Micah 5:5-6).

He is from the Revived Grecian Empire and a native Jew by birth, who disregards the God of his fathers: "For I have bent Judah for me, I have filled the bow with Ephraim; and I will stir up thy sons, O Zion, against thy sons, O Greece, and will make thee as the sword of a mighty man." (Zechariah 9:13)

> "He will show no regard for the gods of his ances-
> tors or for the one desired by women, nor will he
> regard any god, but will exalt himself above them
> all. Instead of them, he will honor a god of for-
> tresses; a god unknown to his ancestors he will
> honor with gold and silver, with precious stones
> and costly gifts." (Daniel 11:37 NIV)

> "I have come in my Father's name, and you do not
> receive me. If another comes in his own name, you
> will receive him." (John 5:43) Revelation 13:1-7.

The prophecy of Jacob in Genesis Pointed to the role of One Tribe against All Israelites:

"Dan shall judge his people, as one of the tribes of Israel. Dan shall be a serpent by the way, an adder in the path that bitten the horse heels, so that his rider shall fall backward." (Genesis 49:16-17 KJV). This is very deep prophecy concerning Dan, yet it is clear in the sense that, if Dan shall be a serpent then it means he will be his own brother's devil against them in the future. Thus, how the Antichrist will be a Jew.

Again, Dan as a serpent is a prophetic symbol of Satan and his agent, the Antichrist who will persecute Israel in the time of the Gentiles. In Luke 4 Satan offered his throne (power) and demanded to be worshiped by Jesus Christ who refused and rebuked him instead.

> "And the devil took him up and showed him all the
> kingdoms of the world in a moment of time, and
> said to him, "To you I will give all this authority
> and their glory, for it has been delivered to me, and
> I give it to whom I will. If you, then, will worship

me, it will all be yours." And Jesus answered him,
"It is written, you shall worship the Lord your God,
and him only shall you serve.'" (Luke 4:5-8)

Jesus said of the future tribulation "Therefore when you see the abomination of desolation spoken of by Daniel the prophet, standing in the holy place "whoever reads, let him understand." (Matthew 24:15 NKJV) The Antichrist will do exactly what he had wanted Jesus Christ to do by worshipping him in the new and the third Temple of Jerusalem in Israel. "Do not trust in a friend; Do not put your confidence in a companion; Guard the doors of your mouth. From her who lies in your bosom. For son dishonors father, Daughter rises against her mother, Daughter-in-law against her mother-in-law; A man's enemies are the men of his own household." (Micah 7:5-6)

The Future enemy of Israel will be of their own brothers, Dan. Let's also compare the prophecy of Moses blessing to Dan (Deuteronomy 33:22 with 1 Peter 5:8-10):

> "And of Dan he said: "Dan is a lion's whelp; He shall leap from Bashan." (Deuteronomy 33:22 NKJV)

> "Be sober; be vigilant; because your adversary the devil walks about like a roaring lion, seeking whom he may devour. Resist him, steadfast in the faith, knowing that the same sufferings are experienced by your brotherhood in the world. But may the God of all grace, who called us to His eternal glory by Christ Jesus, after you have suffered a while, perfect, establish, strengthen, and settle you." (1 Peter 5:8-10 NKJV)

The Great Tribulation – Revelation 6:1-19-21

1. The Time and Length of the Tribulation

The whole period of the Antichrist reign of 7 years, (or 1260 days or 42 months) will be the Great Tribulation.

The Tribulation will begin to affect Israel before the Seventieth Week begins; how long is not certain, but when the Antichrist rises at the beginning of the week, Israel will be undergoing persecution by the whore and the ten kings of revised Rome who are dominated by the whore until the middle of the week. The Antichrist will come out of one the ten kingdoms mentioned before, and he will make seven years covenant with Israel assuring them of protection in their continued establishment as a nation (Daniel 9:27). The Jews will not accept Catholicism when it again dominates the nations of the old world and begins to murder all heretics as it has done in the past. Because the Jews will not submit, there will be a widespread persecution of the Jews and "they shall be hated of all nations" during the time of "the beginning of sorrows" when the Antichrist will be endeavoring to conquer all these nations. (Matthew 24:4-12). The Antichrist will need Jewish moral and financial support to help him over these nations, so he will make an alliance with them for seven years. Therefore, the time of the Tribulation is during the whole of Daniel's Seventieth Week (Daniel 9:27). It ends at the second advent (Matthew 24:29-39).

2. Two Divisions of the Tribulation

(i). The First Division

This starts in the first 3½ years of the 70th Week and is termed "the Lesser Tribulation," for it is not as great in severity as the last 3½ years, because of the protection of Israel by the Antichrist during that time. Israel's persecution then will be from a source entirely different from that of the last division. In the later years she will be persecuted by the whore and the ten kings as stated above. This division of the tribulation takes in the fulfillment of Revelation 6:1-9:21. The judgments of the sixth seal and first six trumpets comes in this period, thus proving tribulation during this time.

(ii). The Last Division

This takes in the last 3½ years of the 70th Week and is termed "the Great Tribulation," because it will be more severe in persecution upon Israel than the first 3½ years. The Antichrist, who will protect Israel the first 3½ years will break his covenant with her in the middle of the Week and become her most bitter enemy. He will then try to destroy her, which calls for the judgment of the seven vials of the last 3½ years. This part of the tribulation includes the fulfillment of Revelation 10:1-19:21. Jesus, Daniel, Jeremiah, and many others speak of this time of Israel's trouble as being worse than any time that has ever been on Earth or will be.

Jesus – Matthew 24:21-22.
John – Revelation 11:1-2; 12:14-17; 13:5-7
Jeremiah – 30:4-11;
Daniel 12:1

3. The Purpose of the Tribulation

1. To purify Israel and bring her people back to a place where God can fulfill the everlasting covenants made with their fathers. (Isaiah 2:6; 3:26; 16:1-5; 24:1-25; 26:20-21; Ezekiel 20:33-34; 22:17-22; Romans 11:25-29).

2. To purify Israel of all rebellion. (Ezekiel 20:33-34; 22:17-22: Zechariah 13:8-9; Malachi 3:3-4).

3. To plead with and bring Israel into the bond of new covenant. (Ezekiel 20:33-34; 36:24-28; Jeremiah 30:3-11; Zechariah 12:10-13:9; Malachi 4:3-4).

4. To judge Israel and punish her people for their rejection of the Messiah and make them willing to accept Him when He comes the second time. (Ezekiel 20:33-34; Zechariah 12:10-13:9; 14:1-15; Matthew 24:15-31).

5. To judge the nations for their persecution of Israel. (Isaiah 63:1-5; Joel 3; Revelation 6:1-19:21).

6. To bring Israel to complete repentance. (Zechariah 12:10-13:9; Romans 11:26-29; Matthew 23:39)

7. To fulfill the prophecies of Daniel. (Daniel 9:24-27; Revelation 6:1-19:21; Matthew 24:15, 29).

8. To cause Israel to flee into the wilderness of Edom and Moab and to be so persecuted by the nations that Israel will have to turn to God for help. (Isaiah 16:1-5; Ezekiel 20:33-35; Daniel 11:40-12:7; Hosea 2:14-17; Matthew 24:15-31; Revelation 12).

4. The Character of the Tribulation

The character of the Tribulation can easily be understood in view of God's wrath being poured out upon mankind for their wickedness and corruption which will exceed the days of Noah and Lot. (Genesis 6; Matthew 24:37-39; Luke 17:22-37; 2 Timothy 3:1-12).

Men will still reject the truth until God turns them over to the "strong delusion" of the Anti-Christ who will cause them to believe a lie and be damned (2 Thessalonians 2:8-12; 2 Peter 3:1-9). Even after God pours out His judgments upon men, they will still defy Him. (Revelation 9:20- 21; 6:2-11; 17:1-18; 18:1-24.

Words cannot describe the utter rebellion and wickedness of men during this period of final struggle between God and the devil over possession of the Earth. (Revelation 11:15; 12:7-12; 19:11-21; 20:1-3).

The Two Witnesses

The Forty-Two Months of Revelation 11:1-2

This period wherein the Gentiles will "trample" Jerusalem is, as explained above, a reference to the Great Tribulation (which commences with the seventh trumpet directly after the termination of the two-witness ministry discussed in Revelation chapter 11). Our Lord makes a similar reference to the trampling of Jerusalem by the Gentiles in Luke 21:24, and tells us that this situation of Gentile intrusion and conquest will continue "until the Times Gentiles have been fulfilled", that is, until the second coming of Jesus Christ will bring the Antichrist's control of Israel and Jerusalem to a violent and immediate conclusion. It will be useful at this point to summarize the various scriptural designations for the forty-two-month time covered by the Great Tribulation:

- In Daniel 7:25, the saints of the Most High (believers) are said to be handed over into the power of the little horn (Antichrist and the Great Persecution) for "a time, times, and half a time", a biblical way of expressing the three and one half years of the Great Tribulation.

- In Daniel 9:26, "the people of the prince which is to come" (Antichrist as the ruler of revived Greece) will make a treaty during the last "seven years" and break it in the middle of the "seven years", that is, during middle of the seven years at the outset of the Great Tribulation.

- In Daniel 12:7, the angel speaking with Daniel declares that it will be "a time, times, and half a time" before the persecutions stop and everything comes to an end, that is, the Great Tribulation will last three and one half years.

- In Revelation 11:2, the Gentiles (the army of the Antichrist) will afflict Jerusalem for 42 months, that is, during the entire three and a half year period of the Great Tribulation (albeit under varying circumstances).

- In Revelation 12:6, the woman Israel is said to be protected for 1,260 days, that is, during the whole 42 months of the Great Tribulation (expressed in standard 30 day months).

- In Revelation 12:14, the woman Israel is said to be protected for a time, times, and half a time, that is, during this same period of the Great Tribulation's three and a half years.

- In Revelation 13:5, the unbridled reign of the Antichrist is said to last for 42 months, that is, for the duration of the Great Tribulation.

It is important to note, that the term time is 1 year, and times to be 2 years. So, time + times is like to say 1+2 = 3 and a ½ (half) time making it 3 ½ years.

Analysis of the Two Witnesses

First, let us determine just what Revelation 11:3-13 says about the two witnesses before we examine other scriptures. Any theory of their identity must harmonize with the statements concerning them in Revelation 11. The two witnesses are two men and not two covenants, two dispensations, etc., as is clear from the plain description of them in Revelation 11:3-13 and elsewhere, the truths given as follows:

1. They are my (Christ's) two witnesses (Revelation 11:3)

2. They will be given power from Christ in future (Revelation 11:3). This excludes the argument that they must be two men who have exercised this power in the history.

3. They will prophesy the last 3½ years. All passages referring to 42 months, 1260 days and 3½ years, in both Daniel and Revelation, always refer to the last half of Daniel's 70th Week. Revelation 11:1-3; 12:6,14; 13:5; Daniel 7:25; 12:7. Malachi 4:5-6 prove that the time of the ministry of the two witnesses is before the great and notable day of the Lord, which will begin at the second coming of Christ. This then, places their ministry during the last three and one-half years.

4. These witnesses are to be prophets for they will prophesy for 3½ years (Revelation 11:3). While they will prophesy of the future events, nevertheless, their main purpose will be to preach and turn their hearts back to God and to teach others to avert the judgment of God. (Malachi 4:5-6).

5. They will be clothed in sackcloth as a sign of mourning because of the judgments that are about to fall. (Revelation 11:3–also see 2 Samuel 3:21; 1 Kings 20:31-32; Nehemiah 9:1; Esther 4:1 Psalms 30: 1; 35:13; Jonah 3:5).

6. They are "the two olive trees and the two candlesticks standing before the God of the Earth" (Revelation 11:4; Zechariah 4:3,11-14), showing that two persons are represented. Whoever they are, they were standing before God about 546 BC when Zechariah prophesied, and they were still there when John prophesied about 96 AD. This then excludes the possibility that the Apostle John will be one of the two witnesses, as well as does the fact he was the one who saw them standing before God.

7. They will be given power and the liberty to exercise it at will. (Revelation 11:5-6). If any man desires to hurt the witnesses, fire will come out their mouths and destroy their enemy. In whatever way their enemies may desire to hurt them, they will be killed in like manner. The two witnesses will stop rain during their ministry, turn the waters to blood,

and smite the Earth with plagues as often as they choose. This shows that both are to exercise the same power.

8. When they finish their testimony, they will be placed at the mercy of their enemies. The beast that will ascend out of the abyss will make war on them and will overcome them and kill them, (Revelation 11:7) The phrase "kill them' shows clearly that they will be two natural men who have never died, but who will die at the hands of the beast. If these things are clear, then it is equally clear that they have been both translated to "stand before the God of the Earth" and they are still in natural bodies and will be sent back to the Earth as mortals, otherwise they could never be killed by the Anti-Christ. Nothing is clearer concerning the two witnesses than that they will die as every other man has died. This alone excludes the idea that they have resurrected or glorified bodies in heaven now or will have such on earth during their ministry.

9. When they are slain by the beast, their bodies will lie in the streets of Jerusalem for three and one-half days. Men will not suffer them to be put into graves. They will gloat over their death and make merry because these two prophets who tormented them are dead. After three and one-half days, the spirit of life from God will enter them and they will stand upon their feet and ascend into Heaven before their enemies. This will produce paralyzing fear upon their enemies and in the same hour a great earthquake will cause seven thousand deaths. The rest in awe will give glory to God (Revelation 11:8-13). This is the same earthquake referred to under the seventh vial (Revelation 16:17-21). These facts concerning the two witnesses in Revelation simplify the question as to their identity. In fact, almost everything is revealed concerning them but their names, and thus all speculation on the subject can be excluded.

The Identity of the Two Witnesses

There are only two men in the entire Bible who fit this plain Revelation. They are Enoch and Elijah. That Elijah will be one of them is clear from Malachi 4:4-9. Some think John the Baptist fulfilled this passage because of what is said of him in Matthew 11:14, but he was never Elijah in person, as John himself testified John 1:19-23. Both Christ and John were truthful. When John said that he was not Elijah he meant that he was not Elijah in person, for he could not have been the natural son of a Tishbite in the days of Ahab and also be the natural son of Zechariah and Elizabeth as is recorded in Luke 1. All Christ had in mind in Matthew 11:14 was that John was the one who to come in the "Spirit and power of Elias" as in Luke 1:17. Malachi 3:2-6, 13-17; 4:1-6 have reference to the second advert of Christ because they speak of judgment and tribulation and the day of the Lord, and not of grace as in John's day. Thus, Elijah will be one of the two witnesses who will withstand Anti-Christ as he did Jezebel and Ahab of old.

Enoch will be the Other Witness

Enoch will be the other witness. Enoch and Elijah are the only two men who have not tasted death; that is, they have not died their appointed death on Earth. (Hebrew 9:27). This they must undergo as have all other people. (Genesis 5:21-24; Hebrews 11:5; 2 Kings 2). Both Enoch and Elijah were prophets of judgment (Jude 14,15: 1 Kings 17-18). We know that Elijah was translated to heaven and is now one of two olive trees and two candidates which stand before God. Is it not entirely reasonable to believe that since Enoch is the only other man translated and thus did not see death during his lifetime on Earth, that such was for some definite purpose; that is, to be the other witness?

That both men will come back and die their appointed deaths at the hands of the Anti-Christ is not only incredible but is entirely logical. Some argue that since Enoch was translated he should not see death at all, but these words are not found in the passage in Hebrew 11:5. What is said of Enoch in this verse could also be said of Elijah and yet we know that he is to come back and die according to Hebrews 9:27. Enoch lived a natural life under the law of degradation and was subject to the law of death. He could not possibly escape such law unless he should live at the time of the rapture, when the mystery of men being translated without seeing death be fulfilled. (Corinthians 15:51-58).

Why God in His divine purpose allowed just these two men of all mankind be translated, is because they have divine assignment in the end time.

The Antichrist will be Jewish

(*see also on page 236: **The Antichrist's Appearance Unfulfilled prophecy # 5**)*

The Antichrist will be a Jew, though his connections, his governmental position, his sphere of dominion, will by no means confine him to the Israeli people. It should, however, be pointed out that there is no express declaration of Scripture which says in so many words that this daring Rebel will be "a Jew;" nevertheless, the hints given are so plain, the conclusions which must be drawn from certain statements of Holy Writ are so obvious, and the requirements of the case are so inevitable, that we are forced to believe he must be a Jew. To these 'hints', 'conclusions' and 'requirements' we now turn.

1). In Ezekiel we read: "and thou, profane wicked prince of Israel, whose day is come, when iniquity shall have an end, thus saith the Lord God; Remove the diadem, and take off the crown: this shall not be the same: exalt him that is low and abase him that is high. I will overturn, overturn, overturn it: and it shall be no more until he comes whose right it is, and I will give it him." (Ezekiel 21:25-27 KJV)

The dispensational place and scope of this passage is not hard to determine. The time-mark is given in verse 25: it is "when iniquity shall have an end." It is the End-Time which is in view, then, the End of the Age, when "the transgressors are come to the full" (Daniel 8:23 and cf.11:36 — "Till the indignation be accomplished"). At that time Israel shall have a Prince, a Prince who is crowned (verse 26), and a Prince whose day is said to be come when "iniquity shall have an end." Now, as to who this Prince is, there is surely no room for doubt. The only Prince whom Israel will have in that day, is the Son of Perdition, here termed their Prince because he will be masquerading as Messiah the Prince. (Daniel 9:25) Another unmistakable mark of identification is here given, in that he is expressly denominated "thou, profane wicked Prince" — assuredly, it is the Man of Sin who is here in view, that impious one who shall "oppose and exalt himself above all that is called God." But what should be noted particularly, is, that this profane and wicked character is here named "Prince of Israel." He must, therefore, be of the Abrahamic stock, a Jew.

2). In Ezekiel 28:2-10 a remarkable description is given us of the Antichrist under the figure of "the Prince of Tyrus," just as in verses 12-19 we have another most striking delineation of Satan under the figure of "the king of Tyrus." In a later chapter we hope to show that, beyond a doubt, it is the Antichrist who is in view in the first section of this chapter. There is only one thing that we would now point out from this passage: in verse 10 it is said of him "Thou shalt die the deaths of the uncircumcised," which is a very strong hint that he ought not to die the deaths of the "uncircumcised" because he belonged to the Circumcision! Should it be said that this verse cannot apply to the Antichrist because he will be destroyed by Christ Himself at His coming, the objection is very easily disposed of by a reference to Revelation 13:14, which tells of the Antichrist being wounded to death by a sword and rising from the dead — which is prior to his ultimate destruction at the hands of the Saviour.

3). In Daniel 11:36, 37 we are told, "And the king shall do according to his will; and he shall exalt himself, and magnify himself above every god, and shall speak marvelous things against the God of gods and shall prosper till the indignation be accomplished: for that that is determined shall be done. Neither shall he regard the God of his fathers." This passage, it is evident, refers to and describes none other than the coming Antichrist. But what we wish to call special attention to is the last sentence quoted — "The God of his fathers." What are we to understand by this expression? Why, surely, that he is a Jew, an Israelite, and that his fathers after the flesh were Abraham, Isaac and Jacob — for such is the invariable meaning of "the fathers" throughout the Old Testament Scriptures.

4). In Matthew 12:43-45 we have another remarkable scripture which will be considered briefly, in a later section of this chapter, when we shall endeavor to show that "The Unclean Spirit" here is none other than the Son of Perdition, and that the "house" from which he goes out and into which he returns, is the Nation of Israel. If this can be established, then we have another proof that he will be a Jew, for this "house," which is Israel, is here termed by the Antichrist "my house." Just as Solomon was of "the House of David," so the Antichrist shall be of the House of Israel.

5). In John 5:43 we have a further word which helps us to fix the nationality of this coming One. In speaking of the false messiah, the Lord Jesus referred to him as follows, "Another shall come in his own name." In the Greek there are four different words all translated "Another" in our English versions. One of them is employed but once, and a second but five times, so these need not detain us now. The remaining two are used frequently, and with a clear distinction between them. The first "allos" signifies "another" of the same kind or genus (Matthew 10:23; 13:24; 26:71). The second, "heteros," means "another" of a totally different kind, (Mark 16:12; Luke 14:31; Acts 7:18; Romans 7:23). Now the striking thing is that the word used by our Lord in John 5:43 is "allos," another of the same genus, not "heteros," another of a different order. Christ, the Son of Abraham, the Son of David, had presented Himself to Israel, and they rejected Him; but "another" of the same Abrahamic stock should come to them, and him they would "receive." If the coming Antichrist were to be a Gentile, the Lord would have employed the word "heteros;" the fact that He used "allos" shows that he will be a Jew.

6). The very name "Antichrist" argues strongly his Jewish nationality. This title "Antichrist" has a double significance. It means that he will be one who shall be "opposed" to Christ, one who will be His enemy. But it also purports that he will be a mock Christ, an imitation Christ, a pro-Christ, a pseudo Christ. It intimates that he will ape Christ. He will pose as the real Messiah of Israel. In such case he must be a Jew.

7). The mock Christ will be "received" by Israel. The Jews will be deceived by Him. They will believe that he is indeed their long-expected Messiah. They will accept him as such. Proofs of this will be furnished in a later chapter. But if this pseudo Christ succeeds in palming himself off on the Jews as their true Messiah, he must be a Jew, for it is unthinkable that they would be deceived by any Gentile.

Ere passing to the next point, we may add, that it was the common belief among Christians during the first four centuries AD that the Antichrist would come from the tribe of Dan. Whether this will be the case or not, we do not know. Genesis 49:17-18 may have ultimate reference to this Son of Perdition. Certainly, Dan is the most mysterious of all the twelve tribes. In the next chapter of this book we shall look in detail of the tribe of Dan.

The Antichrist — Arthur W. Pink

http://biblehub.com/library/pink/the_antichrist/i_the_antichrist_will_be.htm

The Antichrist will come from Italy, the Vatican, Germany, Russia or any prominent country today or from Heaven or Hell.

According to Daniel 7:7-8 & 23-24 there are significant clues as to his origin:

"After this I saw in the night visions, and behold a fourth beast, dreadful and terrible, and strong exceedingly; and it had great iron teeth: it devoured and brake in pieces and stamped the residue with the feet of it: and it was diverse from all the beasts that were before it; and it had ten horns.

I considered the horns, and, behold, there came up among them another little horn, before whom there were three of the first horns plucked up by the roots: and, behold, in this horn were eyes like the eyes of man, and a mouth speaking great things diverse from all the beasts that were before it; and it had ten horns." (Daniel 7:7-8 KJV)

"Thus he said, the fourth beast shall be the fourth kingdom upon earth, which shall be diverse from all kingdoms, and shall devour the whole earth, and shall tread it down, and break it in pieces. And the ten horns out of this kingdom are ten kings that shall arise: and another shall rise after them; and he shall be diverse from the first, and he shall subdue three kings." (Daniel 7:23-24 KJV)

He will come from within the old Roman Empire and from among the ten kingdoms that are yet to be formed. This alone would prove that he cannot come from Heaven, Hell, Russia, Germany, Italy or Vatican. According to Daniel 7-9, 20-23, he must come from one of the four divisions of the old Grecian Empire, which will be known today as Greece, Turkey, Syria and Egypt. When Alexander the Great died, his empire was divided into four parts which I have talked about in chapter 4, page 166-167. In Daniel 8:9 it states, "Out of one of them," that is, out of one of these four divisions (four generals) of the Grecian Empire the little horn would come, and this is explained in verse 23 is during the later time of existence of these four kingdoms, a king of fierce countenance would rise up. The four kingdoms of Daniel 8 will make four of the ten of Daniel

7, and the purpose of this chapter over Daniel 7 is to narrow the coming of the Antichrist geographically from ten kingdoms to four of the ten; so we can say that he will not come from any country outside of these four kingdoms. Therefore, because he is coming from one of Greece, Turkey, Syria, or Egypt. He cannot come from Italy, the Vatican, Germany, Russia or some other place many Bible students might propose, for more of these countries were part of the old Grecian Empire or the fourfold division of the Grecian Empire out of which Antichrist must come.

The Antichrist will come from Syria

The book of Daniel not only makes it clear that he will come from the Kingdoms of the old Roman Empire, as in Daniel 7:7-8, 23-24, and Daniel 8:7-9, 20-23, but it also makes it clear that the he will come from the Syrian division of the four divisions of Greece, as plainly taught in Daniel 11. The king of the north of this Chapter is Syria, and king of the south is Egypt. Wars between these two divisions of Greece are pictured in Daniel 11:5-34. Verses 35-45 portray war between these same two kingdoms "at the time of the end" showing the result of the last war between them. It states that the land of Egypt shall not escape the king of the north in this last war, thus, identifying Syria as being the country from which the Antichrist must come.

If the king of the north was Russia as many Bible students now teach, how could Daniel 11:44 be fulfilled? What countries are north of Russia that could fight against her as is required by this verse? There are no countries north of Russia, thus proving that the king of the north could not be Russia. When we understand the reference to be the northern division of the Grecian Empire, Syria, everything in the passage fulfills all of Daniel 8:22-23; 11:35-45; 12:1-7.

He will receive power from Satan.

John goes on to describe the ruler of this vast empire as having power and great authority, given to him by Satan himself (Revelation 13:2), being followed by and receiving worship from "all the world" (13:3-4), and having authority over "every tribe, people, language and nation" (13:7).

One World President is possible

> "What has been is what will be, and what has been done is what will be done, and there is nothing new under the sun. Is there a thing of which it is said "See, this is new "It has been already in the ages before us? There is no remembrance of former things, nor will there be any remembrance of later things yet to be among those who come after." (Ecclesiastes 1:9-11)

In John's vision in the Book of Revelation, the Apostle sees the "beast," also called the Antichrist, rising out of the sea (nations) having seven heads and ten horns (Revelation 13:1). Combining this with Daniel's similar vision (Daniel 7:16-24), we can conclude that some sort of world system will be inaugurated by the beast, the most powerful "horn," who will defeat the other nine and will begin to wage war against Jews (Christians). The ten-nation confederacy is also seen in Daniel's image of the statue in Daniel 2:41-42, where he pictures the final world government consisting of ten entities represented by the ten toes of the statue.

Whoever the ten are and however they come to power, Scripture is clear that the beast will either destroy them or reduce their power to nothing more than figureheads. In the end, they will do his bidding.

From this description, it is logical to assume that this person is the leader of a one-world government which is recognized as sovereign over all other governments. It's hard to imagine how such diverse systems of government as are in power today would willingly subjugate themselves to a single ruler, and there are many theories on the subject. A logical conclusion is that the disasters and plagues described in Revelation as the seal and trumpet judgments (chapters 6-11) will be so devastating and create such a monumental global crisis that people will embrace anything and anyone who promises to give them relief.

Once entrenched in power, the beast (Antichrist) and the power behind him (Satan) will move to establish absolute control over all peoples of the earth to accomplish their true end, the worship of Satan has been seeking ever since being thrown out of heaven (Isaiah 14:12-14). One way they will accomplish this is by controlling all commerce, and this is where the idea of a one-world currency comes in. Revelation 13:16-17 describes some sort of satanic mark which will be required in order to buy and sell. This means anyone who refuses the mark "666" will be unable to buy food, clothing or other necessities of life. No doubt most people in the world will succumb to the mark simply to survive. Again, verse 16 makes it clear that this will be a universal system of control where everyone, rich and poor, great and small, will bear the mark on their hand or forehead. There is a great deal of speculation as to how exactly this mark will be affixed, but the technologies that are available right now could accomplish it very easily.

Those who are left behind after the <u>Rapture</u> of the Church will be faced with an excruciating choice–accept the mark of the beast in order to survive or face starvation and horrific persecution by the Antichrist and his followers. But those who come to Christ during this time, those whose names are written in the Lamb's book of life (Revelation 13:8), will choose to endure, even to martyrdom.

7

The Descendants Of Dan

The Tribe of Dan are the Danes (Denmark) and the Irish

Denmark – of the Tribe of Dan

S ince one tribe of Dan from Israel can be singled out as the enemy from their own house, to be the future persecutor, "devil" and his angel the Antichrist, it is legitimate to make search for the descendants of Dan in our world today.

The tribe of Dan was the group of people who descended from the fifth son of Jacob:

> "Now when Rachel saw that she bore Jacob no children, Rachel envied her sister, and said to Jacob, "Give me children, or else I die!" And Jacob's anger was aroused against Rachel, and he said, "Am I in the place of God, who has withheld from you the fruit of the womb?" So, she said, "Here is my maid Bilhah; go into her, and she will bear a child on my knees, that I also may have children by her." Then she gave him Bilhah her maid as wife, and Jacob went into her. And Bilhah conceived and bore Jacob a son. Then Rachel said, "God has judged my case; and He has also heard my voice and given me a son." Therefore, she called his name Dan." (Genesis 30:1-6 NKJV). This is the meaning of the word "Dan." (Strong's #1777 "judge", To act as judge).

The Twelve Tribes in Canaan

As the Israelites came into the land of Canaan, by drawing lots, certain areas of territory were assigned to each tribe. The tribe of Dan was given a tract of land that was smaller than the other land grants, but it was fertile and had a boundary along the Mediterranean Sea where there was fishing and commerce available to them.

However, the tribe of Dan never fully conquered this area because of a lack of faith in God. This was true of the other tribes as well, as the early chapters of the book of Judges clearly teach and led to a time during the period of Judges where it was said, "In those days there was no king in Israel; everyone did what was right in his own eyes." Judges 18:1–31 tells the story of the people of Dan falling into idolatry. They also did not like the territory that was theirs, so they sent out spies to find a better area. In the north, some representatives of Dan learned of an area where a peaceful group of people lived. The tribe of Dan took things into their own hands and wiped out the people of that land, so they could then move the entire tribe up to a region close to the sources of the Jordan River, just south of present-day Lebanon.

> "And they named the city Dan, after the name of Dan
> their ancestor, who was born to Israel; but the name
> of the city was Laish at the first." (Judges 18:29)

The Prophecy of Jacob

In Jacob's prophecy for the "latter days" (Genesis 49:1), Dan was prophesied to "judge his people, as one of the tribes of Israel" (verse16). Here is an interesting characteristic of Dan. The Pulpit Commentary says, "With a play upon his name, the firstborn son of Rachel"s handmaid, Bilhah, is described as one who should occupy an important place and exercise highly beneficial functions in the future commonwealth, enjoying independence and self-government as one of the tribes of Israel (Herder, and others), and performing the office of an administrator among the People not of his own tribe merely, but also of all Israel." Dan was to be a judge in the other tribes of Israel, yet still be his own separate nation.

Jacob continues, "Dan shall be a serpent by the way, an adder in the path, that biteth the horse heels, so that his rider shall fall backward." (verse 17). The meaning of this prophecy is that he would leave a trail wherever he would go. The evidence of this is clear. Dan's migrations as revealed in the Bible, shows them naming everything after their father "Dan," (Joshua 19:47; Judges 18:12, 27-29).

Dan had but one son Hushim (Genesis 46:26), "These are the sons of Dan after their families: of Shuham, the family of the Shuhamites. These are the families of Dan after their families. "All the families of the Shuhamites, according to those that were numbered of them, were threescore and four thousand and four hundred." (Numbers 26:43).

However, "though this family no doubt branched out into several smaller families, which are not named here, simply because this list contains only the leading families into which the tribes were divided." (K&D Commentary). We see evidence of this in the Bible, like "Aholiab, the son of Ahisamach," (Exodus 31:6; 35:34; 38:23). "Shelomith, the daughter of Dibri, of the tribe of Dan:" (Leviticus 24:11). "Ahiezer the son of Ammishaddai" (Numbers 1:12; 2:25; 7:66; 10:25). "Ammiel the son of Gemalli." (Numbers 13:12). "Bukki the son of Jogli." (Numbers 34:22), and "Azareel the son of Jeroham" (1 Chronicles 27:22). These were the smaller families of Dan via Shuham/Hushim. So, the sub-tribes of Dan are, Shuham, Ahisamach, Dibri, Ammishaddai, Gemalli, Jogli, Jeroham.

The Promised Land

When the 12 tribes of Israel took possession of the Promised Land, the tribe of Dan was allotted its tribal inheritance in the south western area of that land. Dan was situated west-northwest of Judah; Dan's territory extended westward to the Mediterranean Sea, and included the busy port of Joppa, next to modern Tel-Aviv (Joshua 19:40-48).

Now the Danites migrated northwards to Laish, and called the city Dan, after their father, (Judges 18). The northern city Laish, now called Dan, by the tribe of Dan, was about thirty miles inland from the ancient busy port of Tyre. Thus, the ancient Danites must have had frequent contacts with the people of Tyre, which was in fact occupied by their brethren the tribe of Asher, (Joshua 19:29). So since their Israelite brothers occupied the land of Tyre, they had access to Tyre at any time. In 2 Chronicles 2:14 we see Danites dwelling in the city of Tyre. These people of Tyre were a people of sea trade and navigation, (Ezekiel 27). These people built Tyre and Sidon on the Lebanese coast.

Later in the history of the Hebrews, the kingdom was divided after the reign of Solomon. The kingdom split into Israel's ten tribes in the north and Judah's two in the south. The people of Dan were in the northern kingdom of Israel. We learn in 1 Kings 12:25–33 that King Jeroboam was afraid that those who lived in his kingdom in the north would still go down to the southern kingdom to worship at Jerusalem, since that was where the temple that God had authorized was located. So, Jeroboam built two additional altars for the people of his nation to worship. He established worship in the south at Bethel and in the north at Dan. He built a golden calf at each location and instituted special days and feasts when people would meet. Sadly, this man-made worship at Dan has been one of its lasting legacies.

Today, many people follow various man-made religions and are convinced that all ways lead to God. Unfortunately, these groups follow the ways of the tribe of Dan. Proverbs 16:25 tells us that "there is a way that seems right to a man, but its end is the way of death." Jesus taught that the way to God was exclusive when He said, "I am the way, the truth, and the life. No one comes to the Father except by me" (John 14:6). John 3:36 teaches that "he who believes in the Son has everlasting life; and he who does not believe the Son shall not see life, but the wrath of God abides on him." To learn from the mistakes of Dan would be to worship the God of the Bible alone and live for Him by faith.

Tribe of Dan in Our World Today

In the 1200's BC, before Dan went to Laish, in a song commemorating a great Israelite victory, the Judge Deborah lamented that during the battle, the "men of Gilead stayed beyond the Jordan [River], and [asked] why Dan remained in ships?" (Judges 5:17). The Danites were so preoccupied with the sea and sea trade that they chose to remain in their ships rather than help their brethren. So even before the time they went to Laish, the Danites were already engaged in sea-faring activities off Joppa. Where were these Danites sailing to?

In Egypt, many of the Israelites, the Royal Line of Zarah-Judah, Calchol, and Darda left Egypt and sailed into Greece. (1 Chronicles 2:6).The Danites knew that these Israelites were dwelling in Greece, and therefore there is ample evidence that the Danites headed towards Greece as well. The historian C.W. Muller noted that, "Hecataeus [of Abdera, Greek historian, 4th century BC] ... tells us that the Egyptians, formerly being troubled by calamities [the Ten Plagues at the time of the Exodus] in order that the divine wrath might be averted, expelled all the [Israelite] aliens gathered together in Egypt. Of these, some, under their leaders Danuss and Cadmus, migrated into Greece; others into other regions, the greater part into Syria [Canaan]. Their leader is said to have been Moses, a man renowned for wisdom and courage, founder and legislator of the state" (Fragmenta Historicorum Graecorum, vol. 2, p. 385).

A book entitled Hellenosemitica (1965) goes to great lengths to show that the Greek "Hellenes" and the Israelite "Semites" were closely related. This book mentions two branches of the Danites ("Danunians" and "Danaans") and shows that these people once occupied the island of Cyprus. It also mentions the Cyprian "tradition of the Danaan migration from the eastern Mediterranean" (pp. 14, 79). That was the very same area which was assigned to the tribe of Dan when Joshua led the 12 tribes of Israel into the Promised Land!

Professor Allen H. Jones (Bronze Age Civilization—The Philistines and the Danites), traces the Danaans, a name that the famed Greek poet Homer often used for all Greeks, back to the Israelite tribe of Dan ("Danaans and Danites—Were the Hebrews Greek?" Biblical Archaeology Review, June 1976).

In Ezekiel 27, we see Dan with Javan (Greece) having trade with Tyre, "Dan also and Javan going to and fro occupied in thy fairs: bright iron, cassia, and calamus, were in thy market." (Ezekiel

27:19 KJV). It is common knowledge among biblical historians that "Javan was regarded as the representative of the Greek race" (Smith's Bible Dictionary), named similarly to the DAMNONII of Scotland (who lived besides the northern River DON of Scotland) and the DAMNONES of DANNONIA which the name was given to Devon and Cornwall. DANNONIA in Britain was named after the Tribe of DAN. The Tribe of Dan was recalled in the Children of DON in Welsh legend and the Tribe of DANA ("Tuatha de Danaan:) who came to the British Isles (according to Irish tradition) from the Land of Israel via Greece and Scandinavia. The area Damnonia in southern Britain as well as being alternatively called Dannonia was also known as "Defenia". The name "DEFENIA" is like that of DAPHNIA which was the former place of DAN in the Galilee in the Land of Northern Israel. "Daphne"("Defenia") is also a name associated by the Talmud with the Lost Ten Tribes.

In Scotland the Damnonii (of Dan) adjoined the Gadeni probably of Gad. Somewhat to the south (in Northern England) according to Ptolemy was the city of Danum which area was later to be occupied by Danes from Denmark. In this case we see the possibility of a group of Celtic culture descended from Dan who gave their name to the city of Danum being followed by Scandinavians who were also descended from Dan and settling in the same area.

The Mighty Hercules

The legend of Hercules has been told from ancient times till our day today. Many have not made the connection between Hercules and Samson. Yet the similarities between the two are obvious. Samson was a Judge in Israel and was of the tribe of Dan! The Danites when travelling to Greece and having still commerce and trade with Tyre, who were of the tribe of Asher, still communicating with the Danites of the Promised Land knew and heard about Samson, their Judge and all his exploits. Coming back to Greece, the stories of Samson were told. The "Encyclopedia of the Classical World," states, "The tales of his heroic deeds lend to the supposition that Hercules was originally an historic figure." Of course, that is Samson.

Both Hercules and Samson were incredibly strong, both killed a lion with their bare hands. Both were virtually invincible. One important event in Hercules' life involved his escaping from the clutches of a symbolic woman, who is called "Pleasure." This corresponds directly to the troubles Samson got himself involved in with the harlots of Canaan.

In his book, "God's Heroes and Men of Ancient Greece" W.H.D. Rouse writes about Hercules slaying of the lion: "Heracles threw down his bow and arrows and leapt upon the lion's back... while he put his hands round the lion's neck ...gripped the lion's throat with his two hands, and bending him backwards, throttled him. There lay the lion dead on the ground." (p. 59). In our Bible, Judges 13:6 says that Samson tore the lion in two, but the ancient historian Flavius Josephus in his "Antiquities of the Jews" also tells us that Samson first strangled the lion, which is exactly as Hercules is said to have done. I don't even know if there ever were any lions in Greece. The Biblical Archaeologist Magazine somewhat tersely comments, "lions, we may remark are not frequent in Greece." (59:1, p.17). In fact, the Greek myths explain this one away as the offspring of a monster! But whether there were lions in Greece is not important; Hercules needed to find one anyway. Why? Simply because the Biblical Samson inspired the Greek legend called Hercules and provided the basis for his life!

Why is he called "Hercules"? The word Hercules in Greek is, "Heracles," which is virtually identical with the Hebrew plural word for traders, "Heraclim," and Heracles is said to have come from "Argos," himself! The Greek myths tell that the people of Argos are from the Danioi were descended from a patriarch "Danaos" who was the son of "Bela." In the Bible, the Hebrew patriarch Dan was the son of the concubine "Bilhah" (Genesis 30:3-6).

Testimony of Josephus the Jewish historian

The Jewish historian Josephus shows that the Lacedemonian (Spartans of Greece) were Israelites, and therefore closely related to the Jews. Josephus relates an incredible letter from Sparta to Judah: "Jonathan the high priest of the Jewish nation . . . to the ephori and senate and the people of the Lacedemonians, send greeting:

> "When in former times an epistle was brought to Onias, who was then our high priest . . . we have discovered that both the Jews and the Lacedemonians are of ONE STOCK, and are derived from the KINDRED OF ABRAHAM... concerning the KINDRED THAT WAS BETWEEN US AND YOU, a copy of which is here subjoined, we both joyfully received the epistle . . . because we were well satisfied about it from the SACRED WRITINGS, yet did not we think fit, first to begin the claim of this RELATION TO YOU, the glory which is now given us by you. It is a long time since this relation of ours to you hath been renewed, and when we, upon holy and festival days offer sacrifices to God, we pray to Him for your preservation and victory . . .. You will, therefore, do well yourselves to write to us, and send us an account of what you stand in need of from us, since we are in all things disposed to act according to your desires...This letter is four-square: and the seal is an eagle, with a dragon [snake or serpent] in its claws" (Antiquities of the Jews, book 12 chapter 4 sec 10; XIII, 5, 8, emphasis added).

The Lacedemonians received the Jewish ambassadors carrying the letter kindly and made a decree of friendship and mutual assistance with the Jews, and then sent the letter to their Lacedemonian kinsmen.

Another Jewish High Priest, Jonathan, somewhat later than Onias, wrote the Spartans "concerning the kindred that was between US and YOU... because we were well satisfied about it from the sacred writings.... It is a long time since this relation of ours to you hath been renewed, and when we, upon holy and festival days, offer sacrifices to God, we pray to Him for your preservation and victory" (Josephus, book 13, chap. 5, sec. 1, p. 318).

In Ancient Mythology, Bryant relates that Stephanus Byzantium shows that Alexander Polyhistor and Claudius Jolaus also speak of a direct relationship or kinship between the Spartan Greeks and the people of Judaea (vol.5, p.51-52, 60).

The Spartans we have identified as the tribe of Simeon who were prophesied to be scattered all over Israel. Living under the realm of the Grecian Danites, their tribal standard would have been secondary to the main tribal standard of Greece which is Dan's tribal standard.

The Symbols of Dan / The Tribal Flag of Dan

The Seal Josephus mentions is revealing because the tribal emblem or ensign, (Numbers 2:2) of the people of Dan included the image of a "snake," (see article "Flag," The Jewish Encyclopedia, p.405). This symbolism is derived from what Jacob had foretold: "Dan shall be a serpent by the way, an adder [viper] by the path..." (Genesis 49:17). Thus, the emblem traditionally associated with Dan is an "adder biting horses heels" (Thomas Fuller, Pisgah Sight of Palestine). However Aben Ezra, a learned Jewish scholar of the 1600's said that the emblem of Dan was an "eagle with a dragon in its claws'" (Dr. Mortz Lewin, Waren die Zehn Stamme Israel's zu suchen?, p.48; Epshtein, Abraham, Eldad Ha Dani-2).

The Danites leave Greece for Ireland

"The Danites ruled about two centuries until the arrival of the Milesians, which took place, 1000 years before the Christian era.' Thus, the date of the arrival of the FIRST COLONY OF DANAANS WOULD BE 1200 BC, or 85 years after Deborah and Barak's victory, when we are told Dan had ships...The early connection with Greece, Phoenician and Egypt is constantly alluded throughout the Chronicles [of Ireland] and records of the Irish Dannans" (Dan Pioneer of Israel, pp.30-31, emphasis added). This first batch of Danites that went to Ireland were called the "Tuatha de Danaan." The word tuath simply means "tribe", "Tuath... Irish history... A 'TRIBE' or 'people' in Ireland" (New English Dictionary on Historical Principles, vol. 10, pt. 1, p. 441).

The Milesians were a group of people who: "In old manuscripts of Ireland, the Milesians and the Danaans were of the same race. They came in batches from Greece and Phoenicia" (Dan, The Pioneer of Israel, J.C. Gawler, p.30). The tribe of Dan is the Irish and Danish – British-Israeli Church of God. They were the second group of Danites to migrate from Greece to Ireland, via Spain and Greece with the Royal family of David and set up the throne of David at Tara in the days of Jeremiah.

The Third Group of Danites

Now the remaining Danites migrated north 30 miles away from Tyre. These Danites that migrated north to Laish. There they named the city "Dan." (Judges 18:29).

Moses had prophesied, "Dan is a lion's whelp; he shall leap from Bashan" (Deuteronomy 33:22). Bashan was the location of the inland Danites. Therefore, a great many of them must have "leapt" from inland Palestine—as probably the majority would later, at the time of the Assyrian invasions of Israel.

In the invasions of Israel by the Assyrians, they took, "In the days of Pekah king of Israel came Tiglath-pileser king of Assyria, and took Ijon, and Abel-beth-maachah, and Janoah, and Kedesh, and Hazor, and Gilead, and Galilee, all the land of Naphtali, and carried them captive to Assyria." (2 Kings 15:29). This is the same list of cities found in 1 Kings 15:20: "So Ben-hadad hearkened unto king Asa and sent the captains of the hosts which he had against the cities of Israel, and smote Ijon, and Dan, and Abel-beth-maachah, and all Cinneroth, with all the land of Naphtali." Notice that Dan is not mentioned during the time of the Assyrian invasion. Did they "leap" out of Palestine to avoid the invasion altogether? Historical evidence suggests that the inland Danites, "migrated northward into the Black Sea region..." (Collins, LTTF, p.412). One can understand the situation of the Danites. With many of their people gone to Greece and Ireland, the tribe must have been depleted. With the soon coming invasion of Assyrians, they must have thought that if we don't get out of the land, there will be none of us left, therefore avoided (leaped) out of the land escaping the invasion altogether.

In the Black Sea region, they kept the tradition of naming places names after Dan their father. The rivers emptying into the Black Sea region used to be named Ister, Tyras, the Borysthenes and Tanais. After they arrived there, the names of the rivers were changed to Danube, the Dnestr, and the Don (Collier's Encyclopedia vol.17 p.434).

Dan — A Serpent's Trail

Jacob prophesied that Dan would be a "Serpent by the way, an adder by the path," (Genesis 9:16-17) meaning that he would leave a trail wherever he would go. When the Danites migrated to Ireland, they left a trail of names throughout Europe. In Hebrew there are no vowels, so the name Dan is written DN, or its Hebrew equivalent. Thus, words like Dan, Din, Don, Dun, Den, or Dn, correspond to the name of Dan.

Professor Totten declares: "There is no grander theme upon the scrolls of history than the story of this struggle of the Anglo-Saxons westward. The very streams of Europe mark their resting places, and in the root of nearly all their ancient names (Dan, or Don) recall the sacred stream Jordan river of rest— from whose whose hands, so far away, as exiles, they set out. It was either the little colony of Dan, obeying its tribal proclivity for naming everything it captured (Judges 18:1-29) after their father, or else the mere survival of a word and custom; but, none the less, it serves to trace these wanderers like a paper trail. Hence the Dan-ube, the Dan-ieper, the Dan-iester, the Dan-au, the Daci and Davi, the Dan, the Don, the U-Don, the Eri-don, and the thousand other Dans and Dons of ancient and early geography, down to the Danes in Dan-emerke, or 'Dan's last resting place'" (quoted in Allen, Judah's Sceptre and Joseph's Birthright, p.263-64).

Denmark, the name of the modern country in Europe north of Germany, means, literally, "Dan's mark." Its people are called "Danes." In fact, because at one time Denmark ruled all the surrounding region, the whole region took its name from them the ScanDINavian peninsula! Clearly, here are remnants of the people of Dan, who migrated westward overland from the Caucasus to their present location in northern Europe! "According to late Danish tradition... Jutland [the mainland of Denmark] was acquired by Dan, the... ancestor of the Danes" from whom their name derives ("Denmark," Encyclopedia Britannica, 11th ed., vol.8).

The Danes claim the descend from "Dan the Great" meaning Dan of Israel (Saxo Grammaticus; "The First Nine Books of Saxo Grammaticus of the Danish History).

In Ireland, today, we find their customary evidence — their place names — in abundance. Such names as Dans-Lough, Dan-Sower, Dan-Monism, Dun-dalke, Dun-drum, Don-egal Bay, Don-egal City, Dun-glow and Lon-don-derry, as well as Din-gle, Dun-garven and Duns-more, which means "More Dans." It should be plain that the ancient Danites settled in Ireland, and most of them dwell in that land today. (It is certainly no coincidence that the Irish Gaelic word Dun or Dunn means "Judge," just as Dan does in Hebrew!).

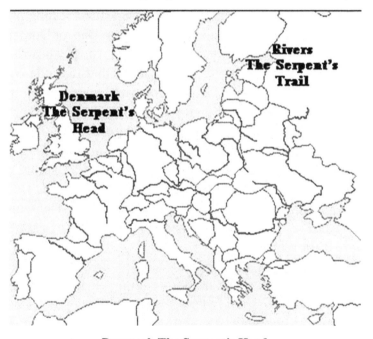

Denmark The Serpent's Head

Prophecy Fulfilled

Jacob said that Dan is a serpent that, "...biteth the horse heels, so that his rider shall fall backward." (Genesis 49:17). Here the

Danites are pictured in the "last days" (verse 1), as under the heel biting the horse. The Irish were governed by the British (the rider) until the early 1920's. The Irish won their independence via a terrorist campaign against the British representatives (i.e. "nipping at the heels") of the British government. The Bible describes the way the Irish obtained their independence. This struggle continues to this day with the IRA committed to overthrow of British rule in Northern Ireland. While not open warfare, "nipping at the heels" aptly describes terrorist actions.

Jacob also says that "Dan shall judge his people, as one of the tribes of Israel" (Genesis 49:16). As quoted from the Pulpit Commentary earlier, Dan would be "...performing the office of an administrator among the People not of his own tribe merely, but also of all Israel." After the early example of Charles Lynch, Irish immigrants quickly found employment in the police departments, fire departments and other public services of major cities, largely in the North East and around the Great Lakes. By 1855, according to New York Police Commissioner George W. Matsell (1811–1877), himself the son of Irish immigrants, almost 17 percent of the police department's officers were Irish-born (compared to 28.2 percent of the city) in a report to the Board of Alderman; of the NYPD's 1,149 men, Irish-born officers made up 304 of 431 foreign-born policemen. In the 1860s more than half of those arrested in New York City were Irish born or of Irish descent but nearly half of the City's law enforcement officers were also Irish. By the turn of the 20th century, five out of six NYPD officers were Irish born or of Irish descent. As late as the 1960s, even after minority hiring efforts, 42% of the NYPD were Irish Americans. Up to the 20th and early 21st century, Irish Catholics continue to be prominent in the law enforcement community, especially in the Northeastern United States. The Emerald Society, an Irish American fraternal organization, was founded in 1953 by the NYPD. When the Boston chapter of the Emerald Society formed in 1973 half of the city's police officers became members.

The Future

The 144,000 of the tribes of Israel that will stand on Mount Zion with Christ when he comes does not include Dan. (Revelation 7 & 14). Why? Some blame it on an ancient scribal error in copying an original document sometime in the far distant past and this error was copied from then until the present. Others say Dan received their inheritance before all the other tribes therefore not listed.

These explanations do not satisfy. Revelation 7:4 says that, "all the tribes of the children of Israel." are listed as the 144,000. So why does it say Manasses instead of Dan? The solution is simple. Dan is split into two nations, Ireland and Denmark. Ireland is Catholic, 80% of the Danes are Lutheran (Church membership 2013 3.1.2013 Kyrkans tidning (Danish); Statistics Denmark Statistikbanken.dk).

Today, the tribe of Dan in Ireland is still given into idolatry following the traditions of their ancestors. They are as a nation, an integral part of the false mystery system God labels as "MYSTERY, BABYLON THE GREAT" in Revelation 17:5. This is a great false church, a worldly church, which has persecuted God's true servants down through the ages (Verse 6).

Notice in Revelation 2:20, this same false church is likened to that wicked "woman Jezebel, which calleth herself a prophetess, to teach and to seduce my servants to commit fornication, and to eat things sacrificed unto idols." God says He will smite her children with death because they have known the "depths of Satan" (verses 23-24).

Jezebel's children, then, are those who have been taught at an early age her abominable idolatries and filthiness (Revelation 2:20) and are deep in her doctrine (verse 24). This woman Jezebel symbolizes the Roman Catholic Church. Most Danites (Irish) are members of this false church from birth, attending her schools, festivals and idolatrous religious worship services. This is the same false church God commands His people to "come out of" so they will not receive of the plagues He is going to bring on those who worship her (Revelation 18 :4). Since the nation of Ireland, the modern Danites, are in the "depths of Satan" and do not know God's true way, probably nothing less than the complete destruction of this false Roman church, combined with the presence and power of Christ's rule on this earth, will finally bring them to repentance. Dan says to God: "I have waited for thy salvation, O Lord" (Genesis 49: l6). It is Denmark that will be part of the 144,000. How can we know? The clue is in the name "Manasses." Back in Judges the 18th chapter the inland Danites who moved to Denmark, when they migrated to Laish and named it Dan after their father. Afterward the children of Dan "...set up the graven image: and Jonathan, the son of Gershom, the son of Manasseh, he and his sons were priests to the tribe of Dan until the day of the captivity of the land." (verse 30). The Septuagint has "Manassas" just like the book of Revelation. (Barnes Notes). God is telling us that it is Denmark and not Ireland that will have 12,000 that will rule with Christ on Mt. Zion. The Irish will have to go through the plagues, watch the Catholic church be destroyed (Revelation 18), and Jesus himself to help them come out of idolatry that they have been steeped into for centuries.

The "day of Captivity" its speaking of is not the Assyrian captivity but, "Most of the commentators suppose the allusion to be to the Assyrian captivity, or primarily to the carrying away by Tiglath-Pileser of the northern tribes of Israel, viz., the population of Gilead, Galilee, and the tribe of Naphtali, during which Laish-Dan was situated (2 Kings 15:29). But the statement in Judges 18:31, "And they set them up Micah's graven image, which he made, all the time that the house of God was in Shiloh," is by no means reconcilable with such a conclusion. We find the house of God, i.e., the Mosaic tabernacle, which the congregation had erected at Shiloh in the days of Joshua (Joshua 18:1), still standing there in the time of Eli and Samuel (1 Samuel 1:3, Judges_3:21 & 4:3); but in the time of Saul it was at Nob (1 Samuel 21:1-15), and during the reign of David at Gibeon (1 Chronicles 16:39 & 21:29). Consequently 'the house of God' only stood in Shiloh till the reign of Saul and was never taken there again. If therefore Micah's image, which the Danites set up in Dan, remained there (if the house of God was at Shiloh), Jonathan's sons can only have been there until Saul's time at the latest, and certainly cannot have been priests at this sanctuary in Dan until the time of the Assyrian captivity.

(Note: The impossibility of reconciling the statement as to time in Judges 18:31 with the idea that 'the captivity of the land' refers to the Assyrian captivity, is admitted even by Bleek (Einl. p. 349), who adopts Houbigant's conjecture, viz., 'the carrying away of the ark.')" (K&D Commentary).

Some of the best commentators, such as Kimchi among the Jews, and many modern era, think it refers to the taking captive of the ark by the Philistines in the days of Eli, because this is the time indicated in the next verse by the mention of the house of God in Shiloh. The ark of God never returned to Shiloh after it was taken thence (1 Samuel 4:3-4) and captured by the Philistines (ibid. verse 11).

Betting the Horses Heels

Today Dan is dominant in Denmark, important in Ireland and Wales, and present amongst the population of the United States of America.

Therefore, the significant of the whole study of the trace and of the tribe of Dan in today's world is to understand that the Antichrist whom will be Jew could emerge from any part of the World.

8

The Timeline of the Bible Prophecies

S tudents of prophecy have concluded that one-third of the Bible prophecy-foretelling of events still remain to be fulfilled in the future. The Bible is the only book in the entire world that has dared to prophesy of events that will occur hundreds or thousands of years ahead. The prophet Ezekiel was called to prophesy of the times that are far off "Son of man, look, the house of Israel is saying, 'The vision that he sees is for many days from now, and he prophesies of times far off.' " (Ezekiel 12:27).

Israel will be Scattered

God has been proven as the "Omniscient," all-knowing of both the past and the future. Thus, God has the infinite awareness, understanding, and insight, possesses the universal or complete knowledge of everything. Fulfilled prophecies of the Bible are proof beyond dispute of the Living God who knows all things from the beginning to the end. There are hundreds and possibly thousands of prophecies in the Bible that have been fulfilled. Every prophecy of the Bible that should have been fulfilled to this date has been fulfilled. To cite just one example, Moses prophesied that because of spiritual apostasy, Israel would be scattered into all nations (not just Assyria or Babylon):

> "Then the LORD will scatter you among all peoples,
> from one end of the earth to the other, and there

you shall serve other gods, which neither you nor your fathers have known, wood and stone. And the LORD will take you back to Egypt in ships, by the way of which I said to you, 'You shall never see it again.' And there you shall be offered for sale to your enemies as male and female slaves, but no one will buy you." (Deuteronomy 28:64, 68 NKJV).

Israel will be Re-gathered

Moses also prophesied that in the end of the age, Israel would be re-gathered out of all nations:

"And you return to the LORD your God and obey His voice, according to all that I command you today, you and your children, with all your heart and with all your soul, that the LORD your God will bring you back from captivity, and have compassion on you, and gather you again from all the nations where the LORD your God has scattered you. If any of you are driven out to the farthest parts under heaven, from there the LORD your God will gather you, and from there He will bring you. Then the LORD your God will bring you to the land which your fathers possessed and you shall possess it. He will prosper you and multiply you more than your fathers." (Deuteronomy 30:2-5 NKJV).

After Moses, prophet after prophet throughout the Old Testament foretold the dispersion of Israel into the entire world, and their return.

Prophecies fulfilled in our generation

1). Hosea prophesied the diaspora would last for 2,000 years: (Hosea 3:4-5; 5:15; 6:1-3; Psalm 90:4).

2). Returning Israel would have to buy back the land: "Men will buy fields for money, sign deeds and seal them, and take witnesses, in the land of Benjamin, in the places around Jerusalem, in the cities of Judah, in the cities of the mountains, in the cities of the lowland, and in the cities of the South; for I will cause their captives to return,' says the LORD." (Jeremiah. 32:44).

3). Hebrew would return as the official national language: (Zephaniah 3:8-10).

Independent State of Israel

4). Israel would be reborn in a day: (Isaiah 66:7-9). In May 14, 1948, the Indecent State of Israel was proclaimed, as the British rule in Palestine came to an end.

May 14, 1948 | Israel Declares Independence
By the Learning Network May 14, 2012 4:02 am

On May 14, 1948, the independent state of Israel was proclaimed as British rule in Palestine came to an end.

Rudi Weissenstein/Israel Ministry of Foreign AffairsDavid Ben-Gurion, the first Prime Minister of Israel, pronounces the Declaration of the State of Israel at the Tel Aviv Museum of Art on May 14, 1948. Above him is a portrait of Theodor Herzl, the father of modern political Zionism.

The May 15 New York Times reported, "The declaration of the new state by David Ben-Gurion, chairman of the National Council and the first Premier of reborn Israel, was delivered during a simple and solemn ceremony at 4 p.m., and new life was instilled into his people, but from without there was the rumbling of guns, a flashback to other declarations of independence that had not been easily achieved."

After World War II and the Holocaust, in which six million European Jews were killed, the United Nations moved to partition Palestine into Arab and Jewish sections. The United Nations adopted the partition plan in November 1947. This plan outraged Arabs and sparked a civil war in Palestine. The Palestinian Arabs had greater numbers, but the Israelis were better armed and organized, and were able to overcome the Arabs. During this time, hundreds of thousands of Palestinian Arabs chose to or were forced to evacuate their homes.

The violence caused the United States to withdraw its support for partition. However, when Israel declared its independence, the United States immediately recognized the new state. The Times wrote, "In one of the most hopeful periods of their troubled history the Jewish people here gave a sigh of relief and took a new hold on life when they learned that the greatest national power had accepted them into the international fraternity."

The armies of Egypt, Iraq, Jordan, Lebanon and Syria invaded almost immediately after the May 14 declaration of nationhood and the withdrawal of British troops, sparking the Arab-Israeli War. Israeli forces defeated the coalition by the end of the year, and, via 1949 armistice agreements, Israel expanded its borders beyond those established by the original United Nations partition plan.

In 1967, after the Six-Day War, the country took effective control of the Gaza Strip and the Sinai Peninsula from Egypt, the West Bank and East Jerusalem from Jordan, and the Golan Heights from Syria.

The political borders of Israel have continued to change over the course of its statehood due to military and diplomatic developments. Today, the country borders Lebanon in the north, Syria in the northeast, Jordan and the West Bank in the east, the Gaza Strip and Egypt in the southwest.

Prophecy of Three World Leaders

5). At the time of the return, three world leaders would die in one month:

"I dismissed the three shepherds in one month. My soul loathed them, and their soul also abhorred me. (Zechariah 11:8). The prophet Zachariah used a metaphor to describe three world known leaders as shepherds.

a). Adolf Hitler was an Austrian-born German politician who was the leader of the Nazi Party, Chancellor of Germany from 1933 to 1945, and Fuehrer of Nazi Germany from 1934 to 1945. He died April 30, 1945, Berlin, Germany.

His primary rules were: never allow the public to cool off; never admit a fault or wrong; never concede that there may be some good in your enemy; never leave room for alternatives; never accept blame; concentrate on one enemy at a time and blame him for everything that goes wrong; people will believe a big lie sooner than a little one; and if you repeat it frequently enough people will sooner or later believe it.

Quotes:

* "He alone, who owns the youth, gains the future."

* "Make the lie big, make it simple, keep saying it, and eventually they will believe it."

* "Those who want to live, let them fight, and those who do not want to fight in this world of eternal struggle do not deserve to live."

* "The victor will never be asked if he told the truth."

* "I do not see why man should not be just as cruel as nature."

* "By the skillful and sustained use of propaganda, one can make a people see even heaven as hell or an extremely wretched life as paradise."

* "Demoralize the enemy from within by surprise, terror, sabotage, assassination. This is the war of the future."

* "It is not truth that matters, but victory."

* "All propaganda must be popular and has to accommodate itself to the comprehension of the least intelligent of those whom it seeks to reach."

Read more at:
http://www.azquotes.com/author/6758-Adolf_Hitler

b). Benito Mussolini was an Italian politician, journalist, and leader of the National Fascist Party, ruling the country as Prime Minister from 1922 until his ousting in 1943. He died April 28, 1945.

Quotes:

* "Democracy is beautiful in theory; in practice it is a fallacy. You in America will see that someday."

* "The truth is that men are tired of liberty. Let us have a dagger between our teeth, a bomb in our hands, and an infinite scorn in our hearts."

* "It's good to trust others but, not to do so is much better."

* "The mass, whether it be a crowd or an army, is vile."

Read more at:
https://www.brainyquote.com/authors/benito_mussolini

c). Franklin D Roosevelt, commonly known as FDR, was an American statesman and political leader who served as the President of the United States from 1933 to 1945. He died April 12, 1945. Warm Spring, Georgia Atlanta, U.S.A.

Quotes:

* "The test of our progress is not whether we add more to the abundance of those who have much; it is whether we provide enough for those who have too little."

* "The only thing we must fear is fear itself."

* "Happiness lies in the joy of achievement and the thrill of creative effort."

* "We have always held to the hope, the belief, the conviction that there is a better life, a better world, beyond the horizon."

Read more at:
https://www.brainyquote.com/lists/authors/top_10_franklin_d_roosevelt_quotes

All three of these world's leaders died in one month in 1945. Thus was the prophecy of Zechariah 11:8 fulfilled.

6). The Order of the return would be:

East (The Middle East); West (Europe); North (Russia); and South (Ethiopia) (Isaiah 43:3-22). The return was in this exact order.

7). Cities of Israel renamed according to Biblical Names:

> "And I will multiply upon you man and beast; and they shall increase and bear young; I will make you inhabited as in former times and do better for you

than at your beginnings. Then you shall know that I am the LORD; for I will take you from among the nations, gather you out of all countries, and bring you into your own land." (Ezekiel 36:11, 24 NKJV).

8). Desolate land to become again abundantly productive and fruitful.

"Those who come He shall cause to take root in Jacob; Israel shall blossom and bud and fill the face of the world with fruit; You shall no longer be termed Forsaken, nor shall your land any more be termed Desolate; But you shall be called Hephzibah, and your land Beulah; For the LORD delights in you, and your land shall be married." (Isaiah 27:6; 62:4 NKJV).

9). Scientific irrigation resulting in annual crop rotation: (Amos 9:11-15)

10). Once barren mountains of Israel to be covered with many varieties of trees: (Isaiah 41:8-20).

11). Vultures to return to await the battle of Armageddon: (Isaiah 34:1-15)

12). Increased rainfall–both latter and former rains restored:

"Be glad then, you children of Zion, and rejoice in the LORD your God; For He has given you the formerrain faithfully, And He will cause the rain to come down for you–The former rain, And the latter rain in the first month." (Joel 2:23 NKJV)

13). Jerusalem an international problem:

"The burden of the word of the lord against Israel: thus, says the lord, who stretches out the heavens, lays the foundation of the earth, and forms the spirit of man within him: "Behold, I will make Jerusalem a cup of drunkenness to all the surrounding peoples, when they lay siege against Judah and Jerusalem. And it shall happen in that day that I will make Jerusalem a very heavy stone for all peoples; all who would heave it away will surely be cut in pieces, though all nations of the earth are gathered against it" (Zechariah 12:1-3 NKJV).

14). Restored Israel to be a democracy with governors (Knesset):

"And the governors of Judah shall say in their heart, 'The inhabitants of Jerusalem are my strength in the LORD of hosts, their God.' 6 In that day I will make the governors of Judah like a fire pan in the woodpile, and like a fiery torch in the sheaves; they shall devour all the surrounding peoples on the right hand and on the left, but Jerusalem shall be inhabited again in her own place, Jerusalem." (Zechariah 12:5-6 NKJV)

15). The small Israeli army to win amazing victories:

"In that day I will make the governors of Judah like a fire pan in the woodpile, and like a fiery torch in the sheaves; they shall devour all the surrounding peoples on the right hand and on the left, but Jerusalem shall be inhabited again in her own place, Jerusalem." (Zechariah 12:6)

16). Israel to have continued problems with Edomites:

"On that day I will raise up the tabernacle of David, which has fallen down, and repair its damages; I will raise up its ruins, and rebuild it as in the days

of old; That they may possess the remnant of Edom,
and all the Gentiles who are called by My name
Says the LORD who does this thing." (Palestinians).
(Amos 9:11-12 NKJV).

God purposely divided mankind. During the time of building the
tower of Babel, in the days of Peleg, God divided the land mass of
the earth into continents and islands. (Genesis 10:25). According
to (Acts 17:24-27), God purposed to disperse mankind into islands
and continents to establish nations. Nations grew into empires, but
God said that empires would fall and be broken up again into separate nations until His own King of Kings would reign supreme.
The prophetic course of empires and nations is given in the second
chapter of Daniel from the image of King Nebuchadnezzar's dream.

17). Babylon, the head of gold, would fall to Mede-Persia: 538 BC.

18). Mede-Persia would fall to Greece: 333 BC.

19). Greece would be divided into four empires: Egypt, Syria,
Mesopotamia, and Asia. 320 BC.

20). The four-part division of Greece would be absorbed by Rome:
the iron empire, and the last world empire, approximately 165 BC.

21). "The Roman Empire would split and break into chunks." AD 500.

22). The chunks of the Roman Empire would continue to rule the
world until the end of the age: the Spanish, French, British, German,
Portuguese, Belgium, and Italian empires, etc.

23). The separates chunks (empires) would bruise, or war, between
themselves: (Daniel 2:40). English-Spanish war; French and
English wars; Napoleonic wars; World War 1 and 2, etc."

24). In the extremity of the age, the chunks would be broken
into many smaller pieces (Daniel 2:41). Franklin Roosevelt and

Joseph Stalin forced Winston Churchill to agree to a break-up of the Roman colonial system; the number of nations in 1945 of 70 rose to approximately 200 by the year 2000.

25). A combination of European nations within the original Roman Empire would form a revised Roman Empire to bring forth the Antichrist: This now seems to be in process within the E.U. The Revived Greece would be the final stage and head of the Antichrist rule to torture the Jews and anyone who does not pledge allegiance to him.

Prophecies about individual people in the Bible

There are hundreds of prophecies about individuals mentioned in the Bible. In this abbreviated study, it is impossible to pursue this aspect of prophecy to any great degree. However, let us consider the central character of the Bible, Jesus Christ.

Case Study of fulfilled prophecy – Jesus Christ

Scholars have listed over 100 prophecies in the Old Testament relating to the birth, earthly mission, death, burial, and resurrection of Jesus. To list just a few of these prophecies:

1. He would be born of a virgin: (Isaiah 7:14).
2. He would be an Israelite from the tribe of Judah: (Genesis 49:10).
3. He would be from the lineage of David: (2 Samuel 7:12-13).
4. He would be called Emmanuel, "God with us": (Isaiah 7:14).
5. He would be born in Bethlehem: (Micah 5:2).
6. Wise men would worship him with gifts: (Psalm 72:10; Isaiah 60:3-9).
7. He would be in Egypt for a season: (Numbers 24:8; Hosea 11:1).

8. His birth would result in a massacre of infants: (Jeremiah 31:15).
9. He would be called a Nazarene: (Isaiah 11:1).
10. He would make the blind to see, the deaf to hear, the lame to walk: (Isaiah 53:4-5).
11. He would be rejected by his own nation: (Psalm 69:8; Isaiah 53:3).
12. He would ride into Jerusalem on a donkey: (Zechariah 9:9).
13. A friend would betray him for 30 pieces of silver: (Psalm 41:9; 55:12-14; Zechariah 11:12-13).
14. He would be a man of sorrows: (Isaiah 53:3).
15. He would be forsaken by his followers: (Zechariah 13:7).
16. He would be scourged and spat upon: (Isaiah 50:6).
17. He would be crucified between two thieves (Isaiah 53:12).
18. He would be given vinegar to drink: (Psalm 69:21).
19. His feet and hands would be pierced: (Psalm 22:16; Zechariah 12:10).
20. His garments would be gambled for at his death: (Psalm 22:18).
21. He would commend his spirit to the Father: (Psalm 31:5).
22. Although crucified, no bones would be broken: (Exodus 12:46; Psalm 34:20).
23. He would be buried with the rich: (Isaiah 53:9).
24. He would be raised from the dead: (Psalm 16:10).
25. He would ascend to heaven: (Psalm 24:7-10).
26. He would be seated at God's right hand to intercede for us: (Psalm 110:1).

Prophecies Relating to the Triumphant Return of Jesus Christ

There are many other prophecies relating to the triumphant return of Jesus Christ, His millennial reign, and His eternal Kingdom. Therefore, we can be sure that if all the prophecies concerning Jesus Christ at His first coming were fulfilled to the letter, that all the prophecies relating to His second coming will be fulfilled to the letter. The present roster of all the prophecies of the 66 books of the Bible would require a time of considerable length and size. To capture the meaning of the prophetic Word for today, we refer to a listing of those that relate to a contemporary eschatological setting.

1. Increase of wars and rumors of wars: (Joel 3:9-10; Matthew 24:6-7)
2. Extreme materialism: (2 Timothy 3:1-2; Revelation 3:14-19)
3. Lawlessness: (Proverbs 30:11-14; 2 Timothy 3:1-3)
4. Population explosion: (Genesis 6:1; Luke 17:26)
5. Increasing speed and knowledge: (Daniel 12:4)
6. Departure from the Christian faith (Matthew 24:12; 2 Thessalonians 2:3; 1 Timothy 4:1, 3-4; 2 Timothy 3:5; 4:3-4; 2 Peter 3:3-4)
7. Unification of the world's religious, political, and economic systems: (Revelation 13:4-8, 16-17; 17:1-18; 18:1-24)
8. The absence of gifted leadership among the nations, thus making it easy for the Antichrist to take over.
9. Universal drug usage: ("sorceries" here can also refer to drugs) (Revelation 9:21) abnormal sexual activity (Romans 1:17-32; 2 Peter 2:10, 14; 3:3; Jude 18)
10. Intense demonic activity: (Genesis 6:1-4; 1 Timothy 4:1-3)
11. Mass slaughter of innocents (abortion) by unconcerned mothers: (Romans 1:31; 2 Timothy 3:3)
12. Widespread violence: (Genesis 6:11, 13; 2 Timothy 3:1; Revelation 9:21)
13. Rejection of God's word: (2 Timothy 4:3-4; 2 Peter 3:3-4, 16)
14. Rejection of God himself: (Psalm 2:1-3)
15. Blasphemy: (2 Timothy 3:2; 2 Peter 3:3; Jude 18)
16. Self-seeking and pleasure-seeking: (2 Timothy 3:2, 4)
17. Men without conscience: (1 Timothy 4:2)
18. Religious hucksters: (2 Peter 2:3)
19. Outright devil worshippers (Revelation 9:20; 13:11-14)
20. Rise of false prophets and antichrists (Matthew 24:5, 11; 2 Peter 2:1-2)
21. False claims of peace: (1 Thessalonians 5:1-3)
22. Rapid advances in technology: (Genesis 4:22; Luke 17:26)

23. Great political and religious upheavals in the Holy Land: (Matthew 24:32-34)

Other yet to be fulfilled Prophecies

To the above list we can add the development of weapons of mass destruction; space travel; star wars; increase of deceivers and lying wonders; depreciation of nationalism; and a back-to-Babel world government movement. As we consider that over 90 percent of all the prophecies in the Bible have been fulfilled exactly as foretold, the less than 10 percent that apply to the future will also be fulfilled exactly as foretold.

Next we consider seven unfulfilled prophecies in more detail.

1. Middle East Peace Treaty with the Antichrist: Unfulfilled prophecy # 1

We are instructed by Zechariah and other prophets that Jerusalem will be a matter of controversy to all nations in the last days. The only peace that Israel has ever known was in the days of Solomon, and since it became a nation in 1948 there has been no peace, even though there have been more than fifty peace treaties or agreements negotiated and signed, the latest being the Wyes River Memorandum and the Sharm El-Sheik Agreement of October 2000. According to Daniel 9:27, the Antichrist will confirm or guarantee a peace agreement or treaty between Israel and its enemies. However, there will be no peace. In fact, this false peace treaty initiates the Great Tribulation period that will also end with the war of

Armageddon. From current news reports, this treaty could be signed by the Antichrist at any time.

2. The Great Tribulation:
Unfulfilled prophecy # 2

In the chronological order of eschatology, the Tribulation is a seven-year period of war, pandemic plagues, earthquakes, astral catastrophes, and other judgments that will kill approximately three-fourths of the population of the world. Daniel said of this period, "and there shall be a time of trouble, such as never was since there was a nation even to that same time . . ." (Daniel 12:1). Jesus said, "For there shall be great tribulation, such as was not since the beginning of the world to this time, no, nor ever shall be" (Matthew 24: 21-22). The Tribulation period will end with the Second Coming of Jesus Christ at Armageddon.

3. The Rapture:
Unfulfilled prophecy # 3

A major unfulfilled prophecy is the Rapture. 'Rapture' is an inclusive word used to describe the resurrection of Christians who have died in the past, along with the changing of Christians who are alive from mortal bodies to immortal bodies, all rising to meet Jesus Christ in the air, or the heavens (outer space). This event occurs immediately after the Antichrist confirms the peace treaty and the Tribulation begins (Daniel 9:27; 1 Thessalonians 4-5). We believe there is prophetic evidence that the church will not go through the Tribulation, but this is a controversial point on which not all Christians agree.

4. The Judgment Seat of Christ/Bema Seat of Christ:
Unfulfilled prophecy # 4

The Judgment seat or Bema seat of Christ will occur after the resurrection and rapture of the saints, we shall be judged of the things done in the body whether they be good or bad. "For we must all appear before the judgment seat of Christ, that each one may receive the things done in the body, according to what he has done, whether good or bad. (2 Corinthians 5:10) "For we will all stand before God's judgment seatso then, each of us will give an account of himself to God." (Romans 14:10-12) In the context, both scriptures are referring to Christians, not unbelievers. The judgment seat of Christ therefore involves believers giving an account of their lives to Christ. The judgment seat of Christ does not determine salvation; that was determined by Christ's sacrifice on our behalf (1 John 2:2) and our faith in Him (John 3:16). All our sins are forgiven, and we will never be condemned for them (Romans 8:1). We should not look at the judgment seat of Christ as God judging our sins, but rather as God rewarding us for our lives. Yes, as the Bible says, we will have to give an account of ourselves "Be judged according to our works" (1 Corinthians 3:11-15). Next, Verse 17 works are compared to these materials, some become purer in the fire and others are completely burned up by fire. In metaphor, fire will try every man's works. If one's works are gold, silver, and precious stones they will abide the fire and he/she will receive a reward of crown for his works. If they are wood, hay, and stubble, his works will be burned up, yet he himself will be saved from the loss of his soul. (Verse 12-15) Part of this is surely answering for the sins we committed. However, that is not going to be the primary focus of the judgment seat of Christ.

At the judgment seat of Christ, believers are rewarded based on how faithfully they served Christ (1 Corinthians 9:4-27; 2 Timothy 2:5). Some of the things we might be judged on are how well we obeyed the Great Commission (Matthew 28:18-20), how victorious we were over sin (Romans 6:1-4), and how well we controlled our tongues (James 3:1-9). The Bible speaks of believers receiving crowns for different things based on how faithfully they served Christ (1 Corinthians 9:427; 2 Timothy 2:5). The various crowns are described in 2 Timothy 2:5, 2 Timothy 4:8, James 1:12, 1 Peter 5:4, and Revelation 2:10. James 1:12 is a good summary of how we should think about the judgment seat of Christ: "Blessed is the man who perseveres under trial, because when he has stood the test, he will receive the crown of life that God has promised to those who love him."

(A) Judgment of Believer's Works:

1. Subject: Believers (Galatians 6:8; Ephesians 6:8; Colossians 3:24; Romans 14; 2 Corinthians 5:10)

2. Time: Between the Rapture and the Second Advent (Luke 4:14)

3. Place: In Heaven (1 Corinthians 9:24-27; Romans 14:10; 2 Corinthians 5:10)

4. Basis: Works Both good and bad (1 Corinthians 3:11; Matthew 16:27; Romans 2:6; 2 Timothy 4:14)

5. Results: Rewards of Crown or Loss Reward, but never the loss of one's soul for any wrong doings, properly confessed and forgiven (1 Corinthians 3:11-15) this judgment deals with the believer as a servant. (Romans 14; 2 Corinthians 5:10, 11)

(B) Believers will be judged concerning:

1. Doctrines: (Romans 2:14-16; Romans 14)

2. Conduct to Others: (Matthew 18; Romans 14)

3. Carnal Traits: (Colossians 3; Romans 1-2; 8:1-13; 14:1-23)

4. Spoken Works of Our Mouths: (Matthew 12:32-37; Romans 14)

5. Things that affect others: Slander, quarrels, idle words, foolishness, (fully) dishonesty, broken promises, wrong dealings, etc. (Romans 1:29-32; 1 Corinthians 6:9-11; Galatians 5:19-21; Colossians 3; Ephesians 4;1-32; 5:1-33; Romans 12:1-21; 14:1-23)

6. Things that affect themselves: Neglected opportunities, Talents wasted, loose living, lack of spirituality, etc. (Romans 2:14-16; Hebrews 2:1-4; Galatians 5:1-26; 6:1-10; Colossians 3)

7. Things that affect God: refusal to walk in light, disobedience, rejection, Failure to co-operate and yield to spirit, etc. (1 Corinthians 12; Romans 12; Ephesians 4:1-32; 5;1-33)

5. The Antichrist's Appearance:
Unfulfilled prophecy # 5

(see Chapter 6, page 159–The Identity of the Antichrist)
This is revealing of the Antichrist's identity. For the first half of the Tribulation, the Antichrist solidifies his leadership and advantage.

1. He will be a great orator "Then the king shall do according to his own will: he shall exalt and magnify himself above every god, shall speak blasphemies against the God of gods, and shall prosper till the wrath has been accomplished; for what has been determined shall be done" (Daniel 11:36).

2. A political and commercial genius "He shall also enter the Glorious Land, and many countries shall be overthrown; but these shall escape from his hand: Edom, Moab, and the prominent people of Ammon." (Daniel 11:41; Revelation 13:16-17).

3. He may be a homosexual "He shall regard neither the God of his father's nor the desire of women, nor regard any god; for he shall exalt himself above them all" (Daniel 11:37).

4. A clever liar and deceiver, "The coming of the lawless one is according to the working of Satan, with all power, signs, and lying wonders, and with all unrighteous deception among those who perish, because they did not receive the love of the truth, that they might be saved." (2 Thessalonians 2:9-10). At the middle of the Tribulation (after three and a half years), he will gain political and

economic control over the entire world (Revelation 13:7, 16-17), and then demands on penalty of death that everyone worship him as God and receive his mark. (Revelation 13:8; 2 Thessalonians 2:3-4). In the last half of the Tribulation, the Antichrist will be the cruelest dictator the world has ever known.

6. The Abomination of Desolation:
Unfulfilled prophecy # 6.

The Abomination of Desolation is referenced in many places in scripture, four times in the book of Daniel alone. The "abomination" is when the Antichrist stands in the Temple Mount in Jerusalem on worldwide television and declares himself to be God. This will be the ultimate abomination committed in the Temple (Daniel 12:11; Matthew 24:15; 2 Thessalonians 2:3-4). The "desolation" will be atomic wars which follow in which all grass will be burned up; one-third of the trees will be burned up; oceans and rivers will be contaminated; cities will be burned; and nations like Egypt will be so wasted and poisoned that no one can live in the country for forty years (Ezekiel 29:9-11; Matthew 24; Luke 21; Revelation 5-19).

7. The Mark of the Beast: 666
Unfulfilled prophecy # 7

After the Antichrist becomes the dictator of the world and is worshipped as God, he will demand that every person be assigned a number 666 plus 3 digits country code 011 and area code 240, a chip, mark or, a barcode that is tattooed into the skin. Only those who are assigned a number will be able to work, buy, or sell. Only those who acknowledge the Antichrist as God will get the mark, and an attempt will be made to kill everyone who does not have the mark, He causes all, both small and great, rich and poor, free and slave, to receive a mark on their right hand or on their foreheads, that no one may buy or sell except one who has the mark or the name of the beast, or the number of his name" (Revelation

13:16-17). Only in our days does the technology exist to employ and enforce the mark of the beast.

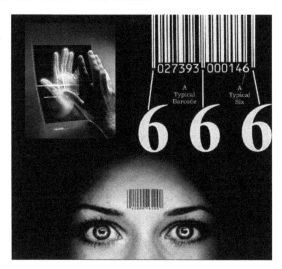

Detail of 666 and the Mark of the Beast

The main passage in the Bible that mentions the "mark of the beast" is Revelation 13:15-18. Other references can be found in Revelation 14:9, 11, 15:2, 16:2, 19:20, and 20:4. This mark acts as a seal for the followers of the Antichrist and the false prophet (the spokesperson for the Antichrist). The false prophet (the second beast) is the one who causes people to take this mark. The mark is literally placed in the hand or forehead and it could be a card. The recent breakthroughs in medical implant chip and Radio Frequency Identification (RFID) technologies have increased interest in the mark of the beast spoken of in Revelation chapter 13. It is possible that the technology we are seeing today represents the first stages of what may eventually be used as the mark of the beast. It is important to realize that a medical implant chip is not the mark of the beast but according to various information sources gathered on the recent mobile chip, in net 10 – 15 years it will be difficult to be employed or buy without RFID chip. The mark of the beast will be an end-times identification required by the Antichrist to buy or employed, and it will be given to all people on earth who want to be employed to make a living or to buy.

1. The barcode of 666

2. The Barcode of 666

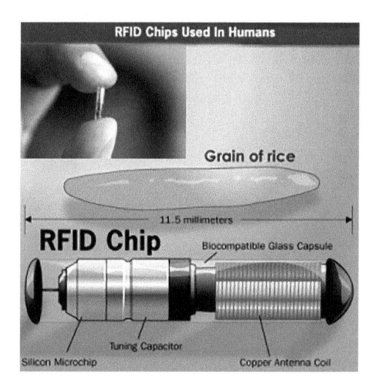

RFDI Chip – (Radio-frequency identification)

What if you were legally required to get 'Chipped' as a Condition of Employment? The Laws are being discussed now

The RFID chip is not a new concept, it was first publicly mentioned in 1950, and then marketed for use on our pets, remember doggy implants?

Now the chips are being used for a whole host of things, besides 'pet tracking.'

We already have voluntary 'chip your employee' programs in Sweden, India, Florida, Oklahoma, California, and the list goes on, and a government agency in Mexico has required it as a condition for employment. Currently, the acclimation process "for chipping" is going on. The attraction and appeal used is convenience, saving lives, payments made easy, being tech savvy and cool. There is no shortage where this technology is being deployed. They are even creating a birth control pill that will use RFID chip technology, football players are using it to track their plays. Driver licenses, credit cards, passports, are all currently using this technology. Using on it items, will make it easy for people to 'accept it on their persons.' And of course, to use it for payments, we will then need digital payments. See where this is all going?

The following questions always comes pouring in when the topic of implantable chips is discussed:

- Do you think they will FORCE people to take this without a choice?
- Do you think they will put it in us without us knowing?

The answer to both is no.

According to Revelation 13:16-18: "And he causes all, both small and great, rich and poor, free and slave, to receive a mark on their right hand, or on their foreheads, and that no one may buy or sell, except one that has the mark, or the name of the beast, or the number of his name. Here is wisdom. Let him that has understanding calculate the number of the beast: for it is the number of a man; his number is 666." (Revelation 13:16-18 NKJV)

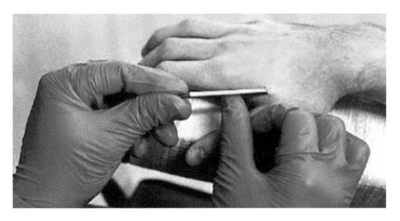

A person getting the chip implanted in their hand.

However, if you do get the mark of the beast, you will forever be sentenced to eternal damnation in the lake of fire.

Revelation 14:9-11

> "If anyone worships the beast and his image, and receives his mark on his forehead, or on his hand, he himself shall also drink of the wine of the wrath of God, which is poured out full strength into the cup of His indignation. He shall be tormented with fire and brimstone in the presence of the holy angels, and in the presence of the Lamb. And the smoke of their torment ascends forever and ever; and they have no rest day nor night, who worship the beast and his image, and whoever receives the mark of his name." Revelation 14:9-11 (NKJV)

The mark of the beast will HAVE to be a choice, your key words are "IF" and "SAVE" = choice! BUT, like all things, that "choice" will come with consequences. Refusing the chip will mean:

Not being able to:

- Buy or sell
- Eat
- Work
- Get Clothing
- Pay Bills
- Have access to Utilities (Water, gas, electric, communication, phone)
- Have a bank account

So, before you voluntarily go offering up your soul as a sacrifice to Satan, I urge you to understand what this mark is. DO NOT EVER put an implantable chip in your body or receive a tattoo (digital that has a chip inside), RFID, NFC, chip on your body, PERIOD. I don't care what the reason is, what the attraction is, it's a trap. PERIOD.

The Meaning of 666

The meaning of 666 is a mystery as well.

Speculations

Some speculated that there was a connection to June 6, 2006 06/06/06.

- **http://archive.boston.com/news/globe/living/articles/2006/06/03/060606__apocalypse_now/**
- **http://www.haunted.com.au/news/age06.html**

However, in Revelation chapter 13, the number 666 identifies a person, not a date. That means, there is a person (a man) who will come and give this number or mark to people. The number of man mean the man Antichrist, who will be the last world leader in our generation.

Revelation 13:17-18 (KJV)

"And that no man might buy or sell, save he that had the mark, or the name of the beast, or the number of his name. "Here is wisdom. Let him that hath understanding count the number of the beast: for it is the number of a man; and his number is Six hundred three-score and six. [666]."

Somehow, the number 666 will identify the Antichrist. For centuries Bible interpreters have been trying to identify certain individuals with 666. Nothing is conclusive. That is why Revelation 13:18 says the number requires wisdom, when the Antichrist is revealed (2 Thessalonians 2:3-4), it will be clear who he is and how the number 666 identifies him.

"The number of men" is just telling you he is a person, who would initiate the process of modern technological system of the 666 number. John said, count the number of the beast. So, it is an alpha-numeric that could be counted and will be given by a person call Anti-Christ.

> "But thou, O Daniel, shut up the words, and seal
> the book, even to the time of the end: many shall
> run to and fro, and knowledge shall be increased".
> (Daniel 12:4 KJV)

Because of the increase of modern knowledge in technology, 666 will be easy to process in such a system that will eventually take the world by surprise. The world today runs by systems of technology, and once the system is programed and accepted, you can't escape it, you have to use it to survive daily life like driving, using ATM, Clock in and clock out at work and credit and debit card, to mention just a few here.

8. The Coming of Elijah and the Two Witnesses:
Unfulfilled prophecy # 8

The identity of the Two Witnesses was discussed in Chapter six (page 170 et seq). Elijah and Enoch are the only two men who escaped physical death by being taken up to Heaven alive. According to the prophet Malachi, Elijah must come back to precede the Messiah when He comes in power and glory to bring in the Kingdom (Malachi 4:4-6). Malachi mentioned Moses also in conjunction with the coming of Elijah, and both Moses and Elijah were with Jesus on The Mount of Transfiguration when He revealed to James, John, and Peter His glory when He would come again. Nevertheless, I strongly believe the other possible prophet to come with Elijah for this special assignment is Enoch. The reason being that both Elijah and Enoch must come to die their natural death at the hands of the Antichrist in the future; both were translated to heaven without seeing death. (Genesis 5:21-24; Hebrews 11:5; 2 Kings 2) "And as it is appointed for men to die once, but after this the judgment" (Hebrews 9:27) they are the only two men, born of a woman, who have never died. This excludes Moses or any other man already dead as one of the witnesses. According to Revelation 11, God will send two witnesses to bring judgments against the Antichrist. They will remain dead for 3½ days for the whole world to see their dead bodies (possibly on television) before being resurrected. (Revelation 11:8-11)

9. Israel's Hiding Place:
Unfulfilled prophecy # 9

Is the flight of Israel in the middle of the Tribulation to a place of safety called Petra or Safety?

> "But the woman was given two wings of a great
> eagle, that she might fly into the wilderness to her
> place, where she is nourished for a time and times

and half a time, from the presence of the serpent"
(Revelation 12:14 NKJV)

Jesus foretold that after the Antichrist commits the Abomination
of Desolation; he will make a final attempt to kill every Jew. To
escape, the Jews in Jerusalem must immediately run for the mountains in the ancient Edom, the city of Esau, the ancient home of
modern Palestinians.

> "Who will bring me into the strong city? Who will
> lead me to Edom? Is it not you, 0 God ..." (Psalm
> 60:9 NKJV) see also verses 10-12; and Ezekiel 35).

The 144,000 Jews Selected and Sealed

The book of Revelation has always presented the interpreter
with challenges. The book is steeped in vivid imagery and symbolism which people have interpreted differently depending on
their preconceptions of the book. There are four main interpretive
approaches to the book of Revelation:

1. **Preterist** (which sees all or most of the events in Revelation as
having already occurred by the end of the 1st century);

2. **Historicist** (which sees Revelation as a survey of church history
from apostolic times to the present);

3. **Idealist** (which sees Revelation as a depiction of the struggle
between good and evil);

4. **Futurist** (which sees Revelation as a prophecy of events to
come). Of the four, only the futurist approach interprets Revelation
in the same grammatical-historical method as the rest of Scripture.
It is also a better fit with Revelation's own claim to be prophecy
(Revelation 1:3; 22:7, 10, 18, 19). So, the answer to the question of
"who are the 144,000?" will depend on which interpretive approach

you take to the book of Revelation. Except for the futurist approach, all the other approaches interpret the 144,000 symbolically, as representative of the church and the number 144,000 being symbolic of the totality, i.e., the complete number, of the church. Yet when taken at face value: "Then I heard the number of those who were sealed: 144,000 from all the tribes of Israel" (Revelation 7:4), nothing in the passage leads to interpreting the 144,000 as anything but a literal number of Jews, 12,000 taken from every tribe of the "sons of Israel." The New Testament offers no clear-cut text replacing Israel with the church.

These Jews are "sealed," which means they have the special protection of God from all the divine judgments and from the Antichrist to perform their mission during the tribulation period (see Revelation 6:17, in which people will wonder who can stand from the wrath to come). The tribulation period is a future seven-year period in which God will enact divine judgment against those who reject Him and will complete His plan of salvation for the nation of Israel. All of this is according to God's revelation to prophet Daniel (Daniel 9:24–27).

The 144,000 Jews are a sort of "first fruits" (Revelation 14:4) of a redeemed Israel which has been previously prophesied (Zechariah 12:10; Romans 11:25–27), and their mission seems to be to evangelize the post-rapture world and proclaim the gospel during the tribulation period. Because of their ministry, millions, "a great multitude that no one could count, from every nation, tribe, people and language" (Revelation 7:9), will come to faith in Christ.

Much of the confusion regarding the 144,000 is a result of the false doctrine of the Jehovah's Witnesses. The Jehovah's Witnesses claim that 144,000 is a limit to the number of people who will reign with Christ in heaven and spend eternity with God. The 144,000 have what the Jehovah's Witnesses call the heavenly hope. Those who are not among the 144,000 will enjoy what they call the earthly hope, a paradise on earth ruled by Christ and the 144,000. Clearly, we can see that Jehovah's Witness teaching sets up a caste society in the afterlife with a ruling class (the 144,000) and those who are ruled. The Bible teaches no such "dual class" doctrine. It is true that according to Revelation 20:4 there will be people ruling in the millennium with Christ. These people will be comprised of the church (believers in Jesus Christ), Old Testament saints (believers who died before Christ's first advent), and tribulation saints (those who accept Christ during the tribulation). Yet the Bible places no numerical limit on this group of people. Furthermore, the millennium is different from the eternal state, which will take place at the completion of the millennial period. At that time, God will dwell with us in the New Jerusalem. He will be our God and we will be His people (Revelation 21:3). The inheritance promised to us in Christ and sealed by the Holy Spirit (Ephesians 1:13-14) will become ours, and we will all be co-heirs with Christ (Romans 8:17).

The Man Child – Revelation 12:5

I will discuss only briefly the various interpretation of the Man Child of Revelation 12:5. Although, there are interpretations such as follows, and the reasons why they could not possibly be the ideal symbol.

1. That the Man Child as Christ
2. The Man Child and the true church
3. The bride part of the Church as the Man Child and some says.
4. The Holy Spirit baptized people as the Man Child.

The Man Child is however, another symbol in the book of Revelation and must be treated as such. In fact, the whole contradiction surrounds the symbol of the woman who gave to the Man Child and that is why I am discussing this with you.

1). The Man Child as Christ

It is believed by some that the man child is Christ because He came from Israel according to the flesh (Romans 9:4-5), because He will rule the nations with a rod of iron (Revelation 19:15; Psalm 2), because He was translated to God (Ephesians 1:20), and because He is called a man (2 Timothy 2:5).

This argument is too general and proves nothing, for every Jew came from Israel according to the flesh. Upon this basis any one son of Israel could be taken as the Man Child. The expression "rod" means authority over the nations, and in this sense every raptured saint will reign with Christ, as proved by the following scriptures in both Testaments.

(a). The Old Testament saints will reign with Christ (Psalms 149:6-9; Daniel 7:18, 27; Matthew 9:11, 12; Jeremiah 30:9; Ezekiel 34:24-25; Hosea 3:5).
(b). The Church saints will reign with Christ (Matthew 19:28; 20:20-28; Romans 8:17; 1 Corinthians 4:8; 6:2; 2 Timothy 2:12; Revelation 1:5-6; 2:26-27).
(c). The 144,000 Jews will reign with Christ (Revelation 7:1-8; 2:5; 14:1-5; Psalms 149:6-9; Daniel 7:18, 27).
(d). The Tribulation Saints and all who have part in the first resurrection will reign with Christ (Revelation 20:4-6).

Therefore, since all saints of all ages will reign with Christ, we conclude that the phrase "rod of iron" in Revelation 12:5 does not prove that Christ is the Man Child any more than it could be used to prove that anyone above-mentioned four companies of the redeemed is the Man Child. All these saints will not have the same degree of rule, nor will it depend on whether they are in a certain company that they will rule but will be given authority in proportion to their degree of faithfulness in the service rendered here on Earth. That will be determined at the judgment seat of Christ. (Luke 19:11-27; Matthew 16:27; Romans 14:10; 1 Corinthians 3:11-16; 2 Corinthians 5:10-11).

The translation Christ is no definite proof that Christ is the Man Child. The angel is not showing John the historical ascension of Christ, which he saw with his own eyes about sixty years previously, but a prophecy that will be fulfilled in the middle of the week as revealed here.

That Christ is called a man does not prove that Christ is the Man Child, for others are called men in Scripture. The Church (Body of Christ) is called a man. (Ephesians 2:15; 4:13).

Hence, we see that all these arguments are too general and cannot be used as proof that Christ, any other individual, or group of individuals is symbolized by the Man Child.

2). The Man Child as the True Church

(a). It is believed by some that the church is the Man Child, and the professing Christians are the woman. It is taught that the church will be caught up out of the mass of professing Christians who will be left here to go into the wilderness, because the majority in Christendom who will not be in the church, and therefore will not be ready to go up in the rapture.

This argument is no proof that the church is symbolized by the Man Child and the mass of professing Christians. Then too, there is no statement or indication to this effect in Scripture. Otherwise it would have been given by school. Neither does such an argument prove that the church is caught up in the middle of the week. The church cannot be caught in the middle of the week, as will the Man Child. This theory, like the one about Christ mentioned above, is out harmony with plain revelation concerning the woman and Man Child.

(b). It is further believed that the sun with which the woman is clothed means the righteousness of Christ, that the moon symbolized the Jewish ordinances superseded by the teaching of Christ, and that the twelve stars in her crown represent the twelve apostles.

This is also without scriptural foundation and really contradicts their own arguments, for the woman cannot be the mass of professing Christians who are not ready to meet Christ or go up in the rapture and still be clothed with the righteousness of Christ. If the professing Christians were clothed with the righteousness of Christ, they would be Christ's, and if they were His, they would go in the rapture along with all other Christians (1 Corinthians 15:20-25; 1 Thessalonians 4:16). Instead of clothing professing Christians with His righteousness, Christ condemns such to eternal damnation. (Matthew 23; Revelation 3:14-17; Galatians 5:19-21; 6:7-8 Romans 8:12-13).

(c). It is argued that Christendom will travail in the middle of the week because of the persecution of Christians by the Antichrist.

This argument cannot be used of Christians, for in no passage do we find any statement that Christendom will travail in the middle of the week or at any other time. If the woman symbolizes the mass of professing Christians, she does not have real salvation, or she would be raptured. People must have real salvation if they undergo any serious persecution. This need not be the case with Israel, for the Jews are to be persecuted in fulfillment of prophecy. They cannot escape the persecution by denying some faith as will be possible with Christians during the Seventieth week, for they will be persecuted because of nationality regardless of their religion.

(d). Some think that the Man Child is the church because the seventh trumpet (Revelation 11:14-13:8), according to their belief, is the same as the "last trump" which is blown at the rapture of the church (1 Corinthians 15:51-58; 1 Thessalonians 4:13-18).

The association of the seventh trumpet with the "trump of God" does not prove that the church is the Man Child. In conclusion therefore, it is clear the church cannot be symbolized by the Man Child, or Christendom by the woman.

3). The Bride Part of the Church as the Man Child

This theory teaches that the Man Child represents the bride part of the church, and that the bride of Christ is not to be the church, but merely a select company of believers, known better as full overcomers, who are outside the church. This theory resolves itself into two questions:

(a). Are the body of Christ and the Church the same?

According to theory they are not the same. However, three definite passage prove that they are the same (Ephesians 1:22-23; Colossians 1:8, 24). These passages state that the body of Christ and the church are the same. There is no plain passage that teaches a different between the church and a bride part of the church. No Scripture ever mention a difference between the body of Christ and the church.

(b). Are there two classes of people in the church, partial overcomers as the church and full overcomers as the bride part of the church?

This theory teaches that there are two classes of people and attempts to create within the church two groups of believers, those who partially live in sin and those who do not, those who partially overcome and those who fully overcome. This class of interpreters uses the seven promises that are made to the overcomer in Revelation 2 and 3, claim that the full overcomers form the bride who will receive rewards and reign with Christ, and that the partial overcomers are to be finally save but have no part in Christ's reign. Let us examine the New Testament books to determine whether there are two groups in the church or not.

A. Paul, in writing to the Corinthians, leaves no doubt with them as to whether they form a part of the body of Christ saying. "for as the body is one (not two parts) and have many members, and all the members of the one body, being many, are one body, by one Spirit are we all baptized into one body". If the body is not one, then we might say that the Spirit is not one. If we can misconstrue such plain language and divide the one body, we can also divide the one Spirit on the same grounds, for the same terms are used of both. Paul continues, "Now ye are the body of Christ and members. And God hath set some in the church, first apostle", etc. (1 Corinthians 12:12-28).

This passage at least, does not advance the above theory that there two parts of the body of Christ.

The truth in all Scripture is that only those that are saved and ready to meet God are a part of the body of Christ. In this connection, there are many passages which teach that there is only one class of people in the church and that these are the ones who overcome sin and live a holy life. There cannot be two classes of such people. Every Christian is an overcomer, and no one is a Christian and save who does not overcome, as is amply proved in 1 John 3:8; Romans 6:16-23; 8:12-23; Galatians 5:17-21; 6:7-8 Hebrews 12:14; Matthew 7:21-23. These passages state clearly that, one is either righteous or unrighteous, save or lost, holy or unholy, consecrated or unconsecrated. There are no half breeds in the body of Christ.

B. In the book of Ephesians, the church is viewed as the body of Christ. The church is what Christ is to present to Himself and not a part of it (Ephesians 1:22, 23; 5:26,27). In this letter, as always, Paul uses plural words such as "us," "we," and "all" in starting truths about the church, which is one. He speaks of the Ephesians as being "fellow citizens with the saints, and of the household of God; in whom all the building fitly framed together growth into a holy temple in the Lord" (Ephesians 2:19-22) "to make in himself of twain (Jew and Gentile) one new man" (Ephesians 2:15; 3:6). "There is one body, and one Spirit, one hope, one Lord, one faith, one baptism, one God and Father of all, who is above all, and through all, and in you all" (Ephesians 4:4-6). Paul speaks of the ministry being given for the perfecting of the saints (not a part of them):

> "Till we all come to the unity of the faith; unto a perfect man" (not one perfect part and one imperfect part), "from whom the whole body, joined and knit together by what every joint supplies, according to the effective working in the measure of every part, by which every part does its share, causes growth of the body for the edifying of itself in love'" (Ephesians 4:13 & 16 NKJV) Those who belong to the body are those who are "created in righteousness and true holiness" and have put off the flesh. (Ephesians 4:17-32).

Paul compares the relation of Christ and church to that of a man and a wife:

> "For the husband is head of the wife, as also Christ is head of the church; and He is the Savior of the body. Therefore, just as the church is subject to Christ, so *let* the wives *be* to their own husbands in everything. Husbands, love your wives, just as Christ also loved the church and gave Himself for her, that He might sanctify and cleanse her with the washing of water by the word, that He might present her to Himself a glorious church, not having spot or wrinkle or any such thing, but that she should be holy and without blemish." (Ephesians 5:23-27 NKJV)

Paul concludes: "I speak concerning Christ and the church." (verse 32)

Christ gave Himself to cleanse everyman and if any individual fails to yield to the cleansing process and live in Christ" he is none of his" (Romans 8:9; Galatians 5:24; 2 Corinthians 5:17), and therefore not a member of the church.

All arguments above are based largely on Old Testament examples of the marriages of some historical characters which are used as types of Christ and the church, or on the details of parables which have nothing to do with the subject. Such arguments are not enough.

In conclusion, the church and the body are the same and that there is no such thing as a bride part of the church, or two classes of saved men in Christ, nor is the church the Man Child. The truth is that not even the whole church is the bride of Christ, for it is a city, the New Jerusalem, and not the church according to Revelation 21:2, 9-10.

4). The Holy Spirit Baptized People as the Man Child

According to this theory it is claimed that the Man Child represents only those Christians who have received the baptism of the Spirit, and that all other Christians compose the woman and remnant who are left after the rapture to go through the Tribulation. The school supporting this theory uses the parable of the ten virgins and 1 Corinthians 12:12-13 in trying to support their position.

> "For as the body is one, and hath many members, and all the members of that one body, being many, are one body: so also, is Christ. For by one Spirit are we all baptized into one body, whether we be Jews or Gentiles, whether we be bond or free; and have been all made to drink into one Spirit." (1 Corinthians 12:12-13 KJV)

Let us examine what they offer as proof.

The passage does not and could not teach the baptism in the Holy Spirit but a baptism in the body of Christ. It shows just how the body is constituted. It is the work of the Spirit to bring the individual into the body of Christ. (John 3:3-8; 16:7-11; Romans 81-4, 9-13; 1 Corinthians 6:11; 12:12,13; Ephesians 2:18; 4:4; Titus 3:5), while it is the special work of Christ to baptize the members of that body into the Spirit (Matthew 3:11; Mark 1:7, 8; Luke 3:16; John 1: 33; 7:37, 38; Acts 1:5-8; 2:1-4; 8:15-19; 9:17; 10:44-48; 11:15; 19:1-6). If 1 Corinthians 12:12,13 means the baptism in the Spirit, it would read, "for by Jesus are we all baptized into one Spirit" but it reads "by one Spirit are we all baptized into one body" The baptism in the Holy Spirit does not place one in the body of Christ, neither does it cleanse from sin. One must be in the body before he can be baptized into the Spirit.

The Man Child – The True Interpretation

We believe that the Man Child symbolizes the 144,000 Jews who are the "first-fruits' to God from Israel, after the rapture of all Jews of the church and the Old testament saints. The reasons for this belief are as follows:

1. It has been conclusively proved that the woman represents Israel. Since this is true, it follows logically that Israel could not bring forth a company of Gentiles. She is sure to bring forth a company and this company naturally will be from those of her own nationality, the Jews. She could not bring forth an individual person. Only an individual could do that. Thus, the Man Child could only represent a company of Jews out of Israel. The woman represents a company of Jews. The "remnant" is a company of Jews, so the Man Child necessarily must represent a company of Jews to fulfill the plain statement of Revelation 12. This alone exclude the theory that Christ is the Man Child. There is no other company of Jews mentioned in fulfilment of Revelation 4-19 in Daniel's 70th week other than the 144,000. Then too, as the salvation and sealing of this company of Jews for protection through the trumpet judgments

are the only ones described, it seems clear that these Jews are the ones to be caught up in the seventh trumpet as the Man Child.

2. We have also seen that the woman cannot be the Spirit of Christendom, the church, and that the Man Child cannot be the church, overcomers out of the church, or any Gentile Christians. Thus, by a process of elimination, we are left with only one group of people, the Jews, from which to draw the personnel of the Man Child. Therefore, what other company could be represented but the 144,000 Jews of Revelation 7 and 14? The Man Child must be limited to one of the four companies of redeemed heavenly saints who are saved in the scope of redemption from Adam to the first resurrection, as enumerated above. These companies are saved, dispensationally, in the order in which we give them. When one company is complete then the gathering of the succeeding ones begins.

3. The Man Child represent a company of living saints only, for the women will travail and bring forth the complete Man Child in the middle of the week. She will not bring forth a partly dead and partly living child. This seems clear from the very language of the chapter. That dragon will be immediately "caught up to God and to his throne." How could the dragon kill the Man Child if it were composed of the dead, or even resurrected people? Such a thing is an impossibility and therefore proves that the Man Child must represent living people only, who will be living in their natural bodies and who will have the possibility of being killed. This eliminates the Old Testament Saints, the church saints, and the Tribulation saints. The only remaining company of redeemed that has not been eliminated, and the only one composed wholly of living saints is the 144,000 Jews. They will be sealed to go through the first six trumpet judgments and will be caught up under the seventh trumpet as the man child. They are seen in Heaven throughout the last three-half years so the must be raptured in the middle of the week. Revelation 14:1-5. By catching them up to his throne. God will supernaturally protect the Man Child or, 144,000 of Israel from the dragon and the Antichrist, when the latter breaks his covenant with Israel in the middle of the week.

10. The Battle of Armageddon:
Unfulfilled prophecy #10.

The word "Armageddon" comes from a Hebrew word 'Har-Magedone', which means "Mount Megiddo" and has become synonymous with the future battle (the last world war) in which God will intervene and destroy the armies of the Antichrist as predicted in biblical prophecy (Revelation 16:16; 20:1-3). The word "Armageddon" occurs only once in the Bible, in Revelation 16:16:

> "And he gathered them together into a place called
> in the Hebrew tongue Armageddon."

There will be a multitude of people engaged in the battle of Armageddon in all over the world, as all the nations gather together to fight against the Jews and Christ.

There are scores of prophecies in both the Old and New Testaments that describe the coming conflict (Zecheriah 14:23; Zephaniah 3:8; Isaiah 65; Revelation 19, etc.). This battle will continue from Megiddo near modern Haifa to Bozrah (modern Beseira) in Jordan, 1,600 furlongs, or 176 miles. The evident purpose of this battle is to destroy Jerusalem and prevent the return of Jesus Christ. However, the entire army is destroyed by Jesus Christ and the armies from heaven. The Antichrist and the False Prophet will be cast alive, without being judged, into the Lake of Fire.

The governments of this world, and their supporters oppose God even now by refusing to submit to his rule:

> "The kings of the earth set themselves, and the rulers
> take counsel together, against the Lord, and against
> his anointed, saying, Let us break Their bonds in
> pieces and cast away Their cords from us. He who
> sits in the heavens shall laugh: The Lord shall have
> them in derision. Then He shall speak to them in

his wrath and distress them in his deep displeasure."
(Psalm 2:2-5 NKJV)

The battle of Armageddon will bring human rule to an end:

> "And in the days of these kings the God of heaven
> will set up a kingdom, which shall never be
> destroyed; and the kingdom shall not be left to other
> people; it shall break in pieces and consume all
> these kingdoms, and it shall stand forever". (Daniel
> 2:44 NKJV)

Prophetically, Revelation shows that at "the place that is called
in Hebrew Armageddon," "the kings of the entire inhabited earth"
will be gathered "together to the war of the great day of God the
Almighty." (Revelation 16:14).

Who will fight at Armageddon? (The Combatants)

This Battle of Armageddon will not be an ordinary battle between
two sets of earthly nations as some teach.

It will be a battle between the armies of Heaven under Christ and the
armies of the earth under the dragon, the beast and the false prophet
(Antichrist) as proved in Zechariah 14, Joel 3, Revelation 19 11-21.
On the side of Christ there will be earthly Israel (Zechariah 14:1-
15), the angel army of God (Matthew 25:31-41, 2 Thessalonians
1:7-10, and the resurrected saints of ages (Zechariah 14:1-5; Jude
14; Revelation 19:11-21).

On the side of the Antichrist, there will be the devil and his angels
and demons. (Revelation 12:7-12; 16:13-16; 20:1-13), the ten kings
(Revelation 17:14-17; Daniel 2:44; 7:19-27), the countries north
and east of the ten kingdoms who will have been recently conquered
by the Antichrist (Daniel 11:44: Ezekiel 38; 39; Revelation 16:12),
and many other nations that will co-operate with the Antichrist.

The Lord Jesus Christ will lead a heavenly army to victory over God's enemies. (Revelation 19:11-16, 19-21) These enemies include those who oppose God's authority and who treat God with contempt with leadership command of the Anti-Christ.

> "So, will I make My holy name known in the midst of My people Israel; and I will not let them profane My holy name anymore. Then the nations shall know that I am the Lord, the Holy One in Israel." (Ezekiel 39:7 NKJV)

Will Armageddon literally be fought in the Middle East?

Yes, because it will originate from Jerusalem with the Jews, but rather than being restricted to one area, the battle of Armageddon will be global, encompassing the whole earth. (Jeremiah 25:32-34; Ezekiel 39:17-20).

The exact location of the valley of Armageddon is unclear because there is no mountain called Meggido. However, since "Har" can also mean hill, the most likely location is the hill country surrounding the plain of Meggido which is in Middle East, some sixty miles north of Jerusalem. More than two hundred battles have been fought in that region. The plain of Megiddo and the nearby plain of Esdraelon will be the focal point for the battle of Armageddon, which will rage the entire length of Israel as far south as the Edomite city of Bozrah (Isaiah 63:1). The valley of Armageddon was famous for two great victories in Israel's history:

(1) Barak's victory over the Canaanites (Judges 4:15) and

(2) Gideon's victory over the Midianites (Judges 7).

Armageddon was also the site for two great tragedies:

(1) The death of Saul and his sons (1 Samuel 31:8)

and

(2) The death of King Josiah (2 Kings 23:29-30; 2 Chronicles 35:22).

What will conditions be like during the battle of Armageddon?

While we do not know how God will use His power, He will have at His disposal weapons such as those He has used in the past, that is: hail, earthquake, flooding downpour, fire and sulfur, lightning, and disease. (Job 38:22-23; Ezekiel 38:19 & 22; Habakkuk 3:10-11; Zechariah 14:12) In confusion, at least some of God's enemies will kill each other, yet they will ultimately realize that it is God who is fighting against them. (Ezekiel 38:21, 23; Zechariah 14:13).

Will Armageddon be the end of the world?

It will not be the end of our planet since the earth is mankind's eternal home. (Psalm 37:29; 96:10; Ecclesiastes 1:4) Rather, it will be used for renovation of this planet to then destroy all evil humanity.

(Reference)–John Gill's Exposition of the Bible (2 Peter 3:7)

"But the heavens and the earth which are now in being, in distinction from, and opposition to, the heavens that were of old, and the earth standing in and out of the water, and the world that then was when the waters of the flood overflowed it: by the same word are kept in store; that is, by the word of God, as in (2 Peter 3:5); and the Syriac, Arabic, and Ethiopic versions read, "by his word"; by the same word that the heavens and the earth were made of old, or in the beginning, are they kept, preserved, and upheld in their being;

or "are treasured up"; the heavens and the earth are a rich treasure, they are full of the riches God, as the God of nature and providence; and they are kept with care, as a treasure is, not to be touched or meddled with at present, but must continue in the same position and use; or they are laid up in the stores, and scaled up among the treasures of divine wrath and vengeance, and will be brought out another day, and made use of, to the destruction of the ungodly inhabitants of the world, and to aggravate and increase their misery and ruin: for it is further said of them, that they are reserved unto fire; for though the world is and has been preserved a long time without any visible alteration in it, yet it will not be always so pre-served: and though it is and will be kept from being drowned by water again, through the promise and power of God, yet it is kept and reserved for a general conflagration; see (2 Peter 3:10; 2 Peter 3:12). And as the old world was put into a natural situation, so as to be drowned by water, there are now preparations making in nature, in the present world, for the burning of it; witness the fiery meteors, blazing stars, and burning comets in the heavens, and the subterra-neous fires in the bowels of the earth, which in some places have already broke out: there are now many volcanos, burning moun-tains and islands, particularly in Sicily, Italy, and the parts adja-cent, the seat of the beast, and where it is very likely the universal conflagration will begin, as Aetna, Vesuvius, Stromboli, and other volcanos; and even in our own island we have some symptoms and appearances of these fires underground, as fiery eruptions in some places, and the hot waters at the Bath, and elsewhere, show; from all which it is plain that the heavens and earth, that now are, are not as they always were, and will be, but are reserved and prepared for burning; and that things are ripening apace, as men's sins also are, for the general conflagration. Josephus F23 relates, that Adam foretold that there would be a destruction of all things, once by the force of fire, and once by the power and multitude of water; and it is certain the Jews had knowledge of the destruction of the earth by fire, as by water: they say F24,

"that when the law was given to Israel, his (God's) voice went from one end of the world to the other, and trembling laid hold on all the nations of the world in their temples, and they said a song, as it is said, (Psalms 29:9), "and in his temple doth everyone speak of his glory": all of them gathered together to wicked Balaam, and said to him, what is the voice of the multitude which we hear, perhaps a flood is coming upon the world? He said unto them, "the Lord sitteth upon the flood, yea, the Lord sitteth King forever", (Psalm 29:10). Thus, hath the Lord swore, that he will not bring a flood upon the world; they replied to him, a flood of water he will not bring, but a flood of fire" he will bring, as it is said, (Isaiah 66:16) "for by fire will the Lord plead, or judge: and hence they speak of the wicked being judged with two sorts of, judgments, by water, and by fire: and, according to our apostle, the heavens and earth are kept and reserved to fire, against the day of judgment, and per-dition of ungodly men; the time when God will judge the world is fixed, though it is not known; and it is called a "day", because of the evidence and light in which things will appear, and the quick dis-patch of business in it; and the "judgment" spoken of is the future judgment, and which is certain, and will be universal, righteous, and eternal, and when wicked and ungodly men will be punished with everlasting destruction: the bodies of those that will be alive at the general conflagration will be burnt in it, though not anni-hilated, and will be raised again, and both soul and body will be destroyed in hell."

https://www.biblestudytools.com/commentaries/gills-exposi-tion-of-the-bible/2-peter-3-7.html

When will Armageddon take place?

When discussing the "great Tribulation" that culminates in the battle of Armageddon, Jesus said: "Concerning that day and hour nobody knows, neither the angels of the heavens nor the Son, but only the Father." (Matthew 24:21, 36) Nevertheless, the Bible does show that Armageddon takes place during 2nd coming of Jesus Christ and towards the end of the 2nd part of Daniel's three and half years.

Armageddon–The Metaphor of the Harvest of the Earth and The Vintage of the Earth

The Harvest of the Earth (Revelation 14:14-16)

The Son of Man is to reap, that is, He is the one who will execute judgment upon the people represented by the harvest. This does not refer to the tribulation martyrs, as some teach, for Christ does not slay His own saints. The 'sharp sickle" is the same as that mentioned in Joel 3:9-14 in picturing the destruction of the hosts at Armageddon. Therefore, the scene must be Armageddon and not of the righteous martyrs, as pictured in Revelation 19:21; Isaiah 11:4; Matthew 13:30 & 39; Jeremiah 51:33; Hosea 6:11; 2 Thessalonians 2:8.

The Vintage of the Earth (Revelation 14:17-20)

The vision of "the vine of the earth" is the same in theme as "the harvest of the earth" above. The "harvest" and the "vintage" are both judgments from God and refer to the future Battle of Armageddon. In this vision another angel is the one to reap, thus showing that the angels will have part in the Battle of Armageddon. (2 Thessalonians 1:7-10)

The vine of the earth will be cast into the "great winepress of the wrath of God." The winepress will be trodden 'without city," referring to the place just outside of Jerusalem where Armageddon will be fought as far as sixteen hundred furlongs or nearly two hundred miles. This is definite proof that the gathering of the vintage refers to the gathering of the nations to Armageddon by the ministry of the three unclean spirits, (Revelation 16:13-16) to fight against Christ at His coming. The winepress with the blood flowing out of it refers to the destruction of the nations when blood will flow as pictured here. This same scene is spoken of in Revelation 19:11-21; Isaiah 14:1-8; 63:1-5; Joel 3:1-21: Zechariah 14:1-21

The Purpose of Armageddon

The purpose of God will be to:

- Deliver Israel from destruction by the Antichrist and the many nations under him. (Zechariah 14; Isaiah 63:1-10)

- Punish these nations for persecution of the Jews. (Matthew 25:31-46)

- Set up a kingdom on the earth with Christ as its head. (Daniel 7:13-14; Luke 1:52)

- Rid the earth of all rebellion and to restore God's dominion on earth as before the fall. (1 Corinthians 15:24-29; Ephesians 1:10)

- Give man one more dispensational test before destroying every rebel on Earth. (Ephesians 1:10; Revelation 20:1-10)

- Establish the eternal perfect state (Revelation 21:1-22:5; 2 Peter 3:10-13).

- The purpose of man and Satan will be simply to:

- Stop God's plan in taking over the earthly governments, and to avert their own impending doom, should they be defeated.

The Length of Armageddon

According to Zechariah 14 the battle will only be one day long:

"Thus the LORD my God will come, and ALL THE SAINTS WITH YOU. It shall come to pass IN THAT DAY That there will be no light; the lights will diminish. It shall be ONE DAY Which is known to the Lord – neither day nor night. But at evening time it shall happen That it will be light." (Zechariah 14:5-6 NKJV)

11. The Second Coming: Unfulfilled prophecy # 11

"Now I saw heaven opened, and behold, a white horse. And He who sat on him was called Faithful and True, and in righteousness He judges and makes war. His eyes were like a flame of fire, and on his head were many crowns. He had a name written, that no one knew except Himself. He was clothed with a robe dipped in blood, and his name is called The Word of God. And the armies in heaven, clothed in fine linen, white and clean, followed Him on white horses.

Now out of His mouth goes a sharp sword, that with it he should strike the nations. And He Himself will rule them with a rod of iron. He Himself treads the winepress of the fierceness and wrath of Almighty God. And He has on his robe and on His thigh a name written:

KING OF KINGS, AND LORD OF LORDS."

(Revelation 19:11-16 NKJV)

The second coming of Christ is the chief theme of Revelation. We shall briefly state the facts as found in Revelation 19:11-21:

1. His coming is from Heaven (Revelation 19:11, 14, compare with Matthew 24:29-31; 2 Thessalonians 1:7 and Daniel 7:13-14).

2. He is riding a white horse (Revelation 19:11).

3. His appearance will be somewhat like that in the first vision, with eyes like flames of fire, and many crowns on His head. (Revelation 19:12 c.f. Revelation 1:12-18)

4. His titles and names are "faithful," "True" "The Word of God," and KING OF KINGS AND LORD OF LORDS," besides a name that no man knows, but He Himself. (Revelation 19:11-16).

5. He is coming with authority and for making war upon the nations and judging them. (Isaiah 11:4; 49:2); of treading them in the fierceness of the winepress of the wrath of Almighty God; (Isaiah 63:3; Revelation 14:17-20; 19:15) and of ruling (shepherding) them with a rod of iron. (Psalm 2:9, c.f. Revelation 2:27; 12:5; Psalm 149:7-9).

6. He will command the armies of Heaven who will follow Him on white horses, clothed in linen, white and clean, which is the righteousness of the saints. (Revelation 19:8 & 14).

These six points sum up the glorious coming of Jesus Christ with His saints and angels to defeat the unholy trinity of dragon, the beast, and the false prophet with their armies, and to deliver Israel and establish a reign of righteousness on the Earth.

Never will there be a more glorious event, or a more beautiful sight than this spectacle of the armies of Heaven clothed in spotless white and in perfect order and rank, following Christ on white horses, and accompanied by heavenly angels, anxious for the fray, to take vengeance on the enemies of God.

The Manner of His Second Coming

There are four Greek works that are used to explain the manner of Christ's second coming which we will consider, together with the main passages in which each word occurs.

1. Parousia – means personal coming, immediate presence, arrival, advent, or return. The word is used in this connection in Matthew 24:3, 27, 37, 39; 2 Thessalonians 2:8; 2 Peter 3:4. It translates "coming" in every one of these passages and refers to the personal appearance of Christ on the Earth.
2. Phaneros – means to shine, be apparent, to appear publicly, be manifest, and be seen. It is only used in this connection in Matthew 24:30.
3. Erchomai – means to go or to come. It is used generally relative to the Second Coming of Christ, as in Matthew 24:30,42-43, 43, 48; 25:13, 19, 27, 31; John 21:23; Acts 1:11; 1 Thessalonians 5:2; Jude 14; Revelation 1:7 etc. The English translation of these passages are "come" "cometh" and "coming."
4. Epiphaneia – means "advent" or appearing, brightness, to give light, or become visible. It is used in 1 Thessalonians 6:14; 2 Timothy 4:1,8; Titus 2:13; Hebrews 9:28. The English translations are "appeared" and appearing.

Jesus said, "If I go away, I will come again." Angels on the Mount of Olives at His ascension to heaven said that He would come back to the Mount of Olives (Acts 1:9-12). Zechariah said at that time the mountain would split (Zechariah 14:1-5; Ezekiel 44:1-3), and the Eastern Gate that had been shut would open. At the Rapture, Jesus will not come to the Earth. At the Second Coming at the Battle of Armageddon, He will come down to Earth, and every eye of every person who survives the Tribulation, including the Jews, will see Him (Revelation 1:7; Matthew 24:27). During the Tribulation, two thirds of the Jews in Israel will have been killed, but after the Battle of Armageddon, Jesus will go to Bozrah north of Petra, and lead the remnant back to Israel (Isaiah 65). Then Jesus will establish His Throne upon Mount Zion in Jerusalem and Judge (rule) the nations with a "rod of iron" (Matthew 25:31-32: Revelation 2:27; 12:5; 19:15).

12. The Millennium:
Unfulfilled prophecy #12

This refers to the thousand year reign of Christ on earth. It is mentioned six times in Revelation 20 that there will be a thousand-year reign of Jesus Christ on Earth over the nations.

This dispensation is called Divine Government because God Himself along with the Son and Holy Spirit will set up a divine government on Earth over all nations forever. The first thousand years of God's reign is called the Millennium which simply means one thousand years. It is mille (thousand) and annum (years).

Scriptural terms for this age are:

1. The thousand years reign of Christ. (Revelation 20:1-10).
2. The dispensation of the fullness of time. (Ephesians 1:10)
3. The day of the Lord. (Isaiah 2:12; 13:6 & 9; 34:8; Ezekiel 30:3; Amos 5:18; Joel 2:1; Zephaniah 1:7; Zechariah 14:1-21; Malakai 4; 1 Thessalonians 5:2; 2 Thessalonians 2:1-8; 2 Peter 3:10).
4. "That day" (Isaiah 2:11; 4:1-6; 19:21; 24:21; Ezekiel 39:22; 48:35; Hosea 1:18; Joel 3:18; Zechariah 12:8-11; 13:1; 14:1-9; Malachi 3:17)
5. "The world (age) to come (Matthew 12:32; Mark 10:30; Luke 20:35; Ephesians 1:21; 2:7-14).
6. The kingdom of Christ and of God (Mark 14:25; Luke 10:11; 22:14-18).
7. The kingdom of Heaven (Matthew 3:2; 4:17; 5:3; 5:10; 5:19-20; 7:21; 8:11; 10:7; 13:43; 18:1-4; Luke 19:12-15).
8. The kingdom of God (Mark 14:25; Luke 10:11; 22:14-18).

9. The regeneration (Matthew 19:28; Ephesians 1:10).
10. The time of restitution (restoration) of all things (Acts 3:20-21).
11. The consolation of Israel (Luke 2:25).
12. The redemption of Jerusalem (Luke 2:38).

This will be the seventh millennium since Adam. During this thousand-year reign, all nations will destroy their armaments and there will be no war (Isaiah 2:4). Leaders of the nations will be required to go to Jerusalem and worship the Lord and learn of His laws. If any go not up as commanded, that nation will be judged (Zechariah 15:16-21); Matthew 25:31-32; Revelation. 12:5). Solar changes in the Tribulation will revert Earth's ecology back to the pre-flood state and people during the Millennium will live to be hundreds of years old (Isaiah 65:25). The Devil will be bound and God's curse upon the Earth for sin will be removed, and the ground will again yield everything that man will need (Ezekiel 34:27; Isaiah 65:25; Romans 8:18-23). The law will be enforced, and criminals swiftly executed (Isaiah 65:20). The Millennium ends with another rebellion of the nations, the Earth and everything in it will be burned up (2 Peter 3:10; Revelation 20:9, 11).

13. The Great White Throne Judgment: Unfulfilled prophecy # 13

The Great White Throne Judgment is the final judgment (Revelation 20:11). The chronology of resurrection for those who inherit eternal life is given in 1 Corinthians 15:23: "Christ the first fruits; afterward they that are Christ's at his coming." However, Paul preceded this revelation with a qualifying phrase: "BUT EVERY MAN IN HIS OWN ORDER." The resurrection of the "saved" is Jesus Christ... all members of the church of the dispensation of grace . . . Old Testament saints ... martyrs of the Tribulation period. "This is the first resurrection" (Revelation 20:5) The saved of the Millennium will live to be almost 1,000 years old (no man has yet to live 1,000 years in the flesh), then they will go into the New Heaven and New

Earth without experiencing death. All the unsaved dead of all ages will then be raised to be judged according to their works. All of those raised at the Great White Throne Judgment without Jesus will go into the eternal Lake of Fire because their names are not written in the Lamb's Book of Life (Matthew 25:41; Revelation 20:12-15).

14. New Heaven and New Earth: Unfulfilled prophecy # 14

The final, unfulfilled major prophecy of the Bible is a New Heaven and a New Earth (Revelation 21:1). Neither the heavens nor the Earth are clean in God's sight (Isaiah 34:4; Job 15:15; 16; Revelation 6:14). At the beginning of the eighth millennium, God who created the first heavens and the first earth with the Words of His mouth will create New Heavens and a New Earth where the redeemed, who had chosen Him because they wanted to, not because they had to, will love and worship Him forever. John, in Revelation 21-22, describes in earthly language the New Heavens and the New Earth where the redeemed will live forever (see also Ephesians 1:1-14). But no language is enough to describe, or our minds able to visualize, the unfathomable beauty and glory of God's new creation. "And the Spirit and the bride say, "Come!" And let him who hears say, "Come!" And let him that who thirsts come " (Revelation 22:17 NKJV)

Every reader can come to the New Heaven and New Earth by receiving Jesus Christ as Savior and Lord. Jesus said, "I go to prepare a place for you . . . that where I am, there you may be also." (John 14:2-3)

9

Reclaiming Jerusalem as the Jewish capital

Moving the US Embassy from Tel Aviv to Jerusalem is not Trumpism, it is Paralleled to Biblical Truth

The study of eschatology and prophecy concludes that one-third of the Bible talked about events that will come to pass in the future End Times. However, it is important to carefully watch and study those prophecies and separate them from Trumpism and politics. When it comes to biblical prophecy, no one can force God's hand to make anything work or happen. God uses people, including unbelievers, to accomplish His purposes, especially when it comes to Jerusalem and the Jews. Biblical history confirms this from Egypt, Assyria, Median and Persian, Greece and the Romans. For example, Nebuchadnezzar of Babylon (Iraq) marched his army to Jerusalem to destroy the temple of Solomon. In 70 AD, General Titus of the Roman Army marched his troops to Jerusalem to destroy the renovation of the temple of Zerubbabel by king Herod. This was in line with, and fulfilled the prophecy of Jesus Christ in Matthew 24:

> "Jesus left the temple and was going away, when His disciples came to point out to Him the buildings of the temple. But He answered them, "You see all these do you not? Truly, I say to you, there will not be left here one stone upon another that will not be thrown down." (Matthew 24:1-2)

The Siege of Jerusalem in the year 70 AD

The Siege of Jerusalem in the year 70 AD was the decisive event of the First Jewish–Roman War. The Roman army, led by the future Emperor Titus, with Tiberius Julius Alexander as his second-in-command, besieged and conquered the city of Jerusalem, which had been controlled by Judean rebel factions since 66 CE, following the Jerusalem riots of 66, when the Judean Free Government was formed in Jerusalem.

Jerusalem riots of 66 refer to the massive unrest in the center of Roman Judea, which became the catalyst of the Great Revolt in Judea.

The Siege of Jerusalem in the year 70 CE

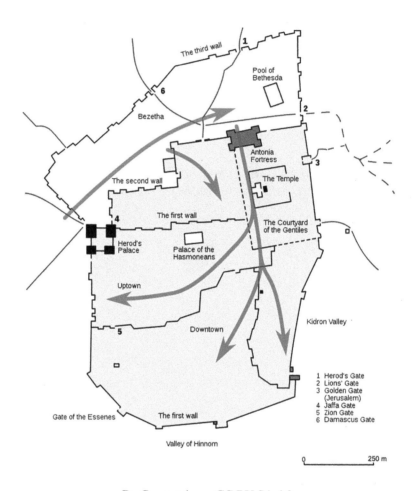

Emperor Titus of Rome

(Titus was Roman Emperor from 79-81. A member of Flavian Dynasty. Titus succeeded his father Vespasian upon his death, thus becoming the first emperor to come to the throne after his own biological father.)
The siege ended on August 30, 70 CE with the burning and destruction of its Second Temple, and the Romans entered and sacked the Lower City. The destruction of both the first and second temples is still mourned annually as the Jewish fast Tisha B'Av. The Arch of Titus, celebrating the Roman sack of Jerusalem and the Temple, still stands in Rome. The conquest of the city was complete on September 8, 70 CE.

Watch this prophecy of Jesus "And they shall fall by the edge of the sword and shall be led away captive into all nations: and Jerusalem shall be trodden down of the Gentiles, until the times of the Gentiles be fulfilled. Luke 21:24. You can see that; part of this prophecy has been fulfilled; (And they shall fall by the edge of the sword and shall be led away captive into all nations: and Jerusalem shall be trodden down of the Gentiles. When was the state of Palestine came into existence? It was after the dispersion of the Jews from their Land in Jerusalem. Read the History of the state of Palestine and McMahon–Hussein Correspondence (1915–16)

https://en.wikipedia.org/wiki/History_of_the_State_of_ Palestine#McMahon–Hussein_Correspondence_ (1915–16)

We are still counting on the Times of The Gentiles to be fulfilled. In between that;

* Jerusalem needs to be reclaimed by the Jews as their Capital.

* The Jews must build the 3rd Temple in Jerusalem at the Temple Mount.

* There will be a continual intifada and eventually the Jews will kill more Palestinian Arabs because of the Dome of Rock that sits at the original temple mount, precisely at the original place of the

Holy of Holies. The above are the all the events that must take place before the coming of Jesus.

https://www.gotquestions.org/Dome-of-the-Rock.html

Israel will be Re-gathered

Moses also prophesied that in the end of the age, Israel would be re-gathered out of all nations. Deuteronomy 30:2-5 (KJV)

> "And shalt return unto the Lord thy God, and shalt obey his voice according to all that I command thee this day, thou and thy children, with all thine heart, and with all thy soul; That then the Lord thy God will turn thy captivity, and have compassion upon thee, and will return and gather thee from all the nations, whither the Lord thy God hath scattered thee. If any of thine be driven out unto the outmost parts of heaven, from thence will the Lord thy God gather thee, and from thence will he fetch thee: And the Lord thy God will bring thee into the land which thy fathers possessed, and thou shalt possess it; and he will do thee good and multiply thee above thy fathers."

To recognize Jerusalem as capital and move the US embassy from Tel Aviv has a biblical truth and should not be politicize. To be clear with this, it is the just moving US Embassy, it is and event that fulfil Bible prophecy of the establishment of Jerusalem and the Jewish Capital. Are we here saying there another way God is going to show Israelites when, how, and who will decree Jerusalem Capital? I think every trustful follower of Jesus Christ need to research the Bible well before coming out with their statements. This is non-evangelical and not conservative or Trumpism issue. The whole truth is in the Bible. Someone could please tell me; how will God fulfil the Bible prophecies in our time here? Does this mean we are forcing the hands of God and the second coming of Jesus, while the truth is in the Bible?

Trump is just an instrument God is using to give the Jews what belongs to them. It is the same way God used the Pharaohs to punish the Jews 430 years. He used Nebuchadnezzar to destroy their temple and sent them in captivity, He used the Romans to scatter them all over the world for 2,000 years until their first return in 1948.

Hosea prophesied that the diaspora would last for 2,000 years:

> "For the children of Israel shall abide many days without a king, and without a prince, and without a sacrifice, and without an image, and without an ephod, and without teraphim: Afterward shall the children of Israel return, and seek the Lord their God, and David their king; and shall fear the Lord and his goodness in the latter days." (Hosea 3:4-5 KJV)

> "I will go and return to my place, till they acknowledge their offence, and seek my face: in their affliction they will seek me early." (Hosea 5:15 KJV)

> "Come and let us return unto the Lord: for he hath torn, and he will heal us; he hath smitten, and he will bind us up. After two days will he revive us: in the third day he will raise us up, and we shall live in his sight. Then shall we know, if we follow on to know the Lord: his going forth is prepared as the morning; and he shall come unto us as the rain, as the latter and former rain unto the earth." (Hosea 6:1-3 KJV)

> "For a thousand years in thy sight are but as yesterday when it is past, and as a watch in the night." (Psalm 90:4 KJV)

Israel would be reborn in a day:

Isaiah 66:7-9 King James Version (KJV)

> "Before she travailed, she brought forth; before her
> pain came, she was delivered of a man child. Who
> hath heard such a thing? who hath seen such things?
> Shall the earth be made to bring forth in one day?
> or shall a nation be born at once? for as soon as
> Zion travailed, she brought forth her children. Shall
> I bring to the birth, and not cause to bring forth?
> saith the Lord: shall I cause to bring forth and shut
> the womb? saith thy God." (Isaiah 66:7-9 KJV)

The state of Israel was proclaimed by the Jewish leader, David
Ben Gurion, on May 14, 1948, and officially came into being on
the 15th, after British Mandatory rule ended at midnight. In many
minds, the birth of Israel is closely identified with the Nazi terror in
Europe and the Holocaust, but in fact the conception of and plan-
ning for a Jewish state had begun some 60 years earlier.

The Messianic idea of returning the Jews to their "promised land"
had been a Puritan religious belief since the 16th Century. In the
mid-19th Century, British politicians saw another value: that of
having in place in the Middle East a Jewish entity sympathetic to
the British Empire.

Two phenomena made real these and the Jews' own previously
vague aspirations of "return": the burgeoning European nationalism of the time, from which the Jews felt excluded; and the massacres, or pogroms, carried out by Tsarist Russia against its six
million Jews, the largest single Jewish population in Europe, which
spread into the Ukraine and Poland.

By the 1880s, groups of desperate Russian and other Eastern
European Jews were settling in Palestine, which was under the
somewhat tenuous authority of the Turkish Ottoman Empire.

http://news.bbc.co.uk/2/hi/events/israel_at_50/history/78597.stm

May 14, 1948 | Israel Declares Independence. By the Learning
Network May 14, 2012 4:02 am.

Index

3. The Great Tribulation – Revelation 6:1-19-21 – page 109-111

4. The Two Witnesses – 112-116

God's plan for man. Expanded index edition – Finis Jennings Dake -Page 792-794

4. The Antichrist will be a Jewish – page 117

The Antichrist — Arthur W. Pink

http://biblehub.com/library/pink/the_antichrist/i_the_antichrist_will_be.htm

5. The Antichrist will Come from Italy, the Vatican, Germany, Russia or From Any Prominent Country Today or From Heaven or Heal – 120

God's plan for man. Expanded index edition – Finis Jennings Dake -Page 300

6. The Antichrist will Come from Syria – 122

God's plan for man. Expanded index edition – Finis Jennings Dake -Page 300

Chapter 7

The Descendants of Dan–page 125-140

https://www.british-israel.ca/Dan.htm

Chapter 8

Independent State of Israel page 146

https://learning.blogs.nytimes.com/2012/05/14may-14-1948-israel-declares-independence/

Adolf Hitler – page 148-149

http://www.azquotes.com/author/6758-Adolf_Hitler

Benito Amilcar Andrea Mussolini–page 149

https://www.brainyquote.com/authors/benito_mussolini

Franklin Delano Roosevelt–page 150

https://www.brainyquote.com/lists/authors/top_10_franklin_d_roosevelt_quotes

The mark of the Beast–7. Page 162

https://www.express.co.uk/news/weird/703856/mark-of-the-beast-secret-plan-to-implant-us-all-with-id-chips-by-2017

666 Speculation – Page 167

http://archive.boston.com/news/globe/living/articles/2006/06/03/060606__apocalypse_now/

http://www.haunted.com.au/news/age06.html

Armageddon, Will Armageddon be the end of the world? Page 182-189 https://www.biblestudytools.com/commentaries/gills-exposition-of-the-bible/2-peter-3-7.html

Armageddon–The Metaphor of The Harvest of the Earth and The Vintage of the Earth – page 188

God's plan for man. Expanded index edition – Finis Jennings Dake -Page 814

The Man Child – Page 180

God's plan for man. Expanded index edition – Finis Jennings Dake -Page 882

By Goran tek-en, CC BY-SA 4.0, https://commons.wikimedia.org/w/index.php?curid=65410812 – page 198

By Sailko–Own work, CC BY 3.0, https://commons.wikimedia. org/w/index.php?curid=30590321 – page 198

https://en.wikipedia.org/wiki/History_of_the_State_of_ Palestine#McMahon–Hussein_Correspondence_ (1915–16 - Page 199

https://www.gotquestions.org/Dome-of-the-Rock.html - Page 200

May 14, 1948 | Israel Declares Independence. By the Learning Network May 14, 2012 4:02 am. – page 203

About this Book

This is a detail and revised model of A Student of Prophecy; now as A Student of the End Time Prophecy.

After 38 years in ministry, I am still asking questions about why over 90% messages in churches, on televisions, audios and social medias are silent about the preaching and teaching of the end time Prophesies? The answers to these questions are my challenged to write this book. This will, however, help shape the minds of fellow ministers, leaders and Christians, who may need such information to preach and to teach as well.

This book is a student's handbook and teaches in-depth knowledge of the end time prophetic interpretation to its readers.

It talks about the things Jesus said would happen before his second coming and the end time prophecies of the old Testament before Jesus Christ. How are they going to happen, where and when are they going to happen and who are going to be used to make them happen? By the time you finished reading this book you will be able to compare and find answers for yourself. (Matthew 24:1-51)

Contact Information

Website: www.hognetwork.org
Email: Kyerenkansah@yahoo.com
        Kyerenkansah2@gmail.com
        Hopeofgloryi@yahoo.org
Tel: +1-347-559-9329

CPSIA information can be obtained
at www.ICGtesting.com
Printed in the USA
BVHW060739171222
654337BV00014B/687

9 781545 673317